"Inkstains on the edge of light" is the second collection of poems and spoken word from Palestinian poet and filmmaker, Hind Shoufani. In four chapters, titled, Death, Life, Home and Lust, Shoufani writes of the Arab world through a cosmopolitan global view, and of the world through her Palestinian refugee identity and rootless lifestyle. She is influenced by the civil rights movement poets and current serious writers of the hip hop generation, specially the influential and powerful poets emerging from Brooklyn.

In over three hundred pages of open free form verse, Shoufani takes the reader on a whirlwind tour of politics, honor killings, terror attacks on Mumbai, lost lovers and new found mourning, sex and humid nights in Beirut, the gulf of Dubai and the dust of chaotic Damascus. She speaks for those who are unnoticed in Arabia. She condemns the labour camps. Sexist mythology. Structures of patriarchy and cowardly lovers. She hurts for and commemorates family deceased, both close and far. She mourns Palestine, a homeland she never knew well. She resists all forms of occupation- both of land and soul. She laughs and sings and dances from throughout the Middle East to her beloved New York. And back.

Praise for *Inkstains On The Edge Of Light*

"Here is a vital, sensuous poetry, international and personal, impassioned and angry, larger than life and cinematically accurate in detail. Hind Shoufani, a polyglot Anglophone Arab poet, a poet of the Palestinian diaspora, is in the line of the Caribbean American June Jordan, the Moroccan Abdellatif La'abi, the British Tom Paulin, the Iraqi Bushra al-Bustani: poets of memory and modernity, protest and passion. But her voice, her cadence, her world-view of a young woman at home and not at home in a dozen cities, are all indelibly her own."

Marilyn Hacker,
Poet/ Educator

"Hind Shoufani has given us a collection of poems that are looking for love.
Her poems long to be held. She dances from Beirut to Dubai. Her lines are borders that we must cross. Shoufani writes with desire. Her poetry is sensual. After politics must come the embrace.
The reader will want to place page to lips. Let the poems of Shoufani kiss your eyes."

E. Ethelbert Miller
Poet/Author/Literary activist

"Hind has a story to tell and this story is essentially personal. But for her Palestine is personal as well. Reading her poetry makes you richer twice. You'll know the woman and the land that the woman does not know because of the Israeli occupation. Almost all the poems are dedicated to other friends from both sexes and from different lands.

Is it the need to communicate? To tell? To narrate? To find a listening ear? Yes.
And this is Palestinian, too."

Mourid Barghouti
Author/Poet

"Hind Shoufani's poems are utterly clarifying. They carry you along on waves of perfectly modulated feeling through perilous landscapes and political catastrophes. They are superb expressions of emotional intelligence. They teach and re-teach the true meaning of love."

Victoria Arana
Professor/ Anthologist

"This is a passionate and intense collection of poems. It ranges from the erotic to the political. What is common among the poems is a sense of deep emotional attachment and political belonging. The poems are not easy: they require attention and more than one reading. The erotic poems succeed in capturing the sexual moment without relying on clichés. This is recommended to those who appreciate poetry and those who believe that our political sides can coexist with our sexual sides."

As'ad Abu Khalil
Writer/Professor/Angry Arab

INKSTAINS ON THE EDGE OF LIGHT

by Hind Shoufani

WHOLE WORLD PRESS

 WHOLE WORLD PRESS

14150 NE 20th Street F1, #305
Bellevue, WA 98007
www.wholeworldpress.org

© 2010 by HIND SHOUFANI.
All rights reserved, including the right of reproduction in any form.

Special discounts for bulk purchases are available.
Please contact Whole World Press at bulksales@wholeworldpress.org
for more information.

www.hindshoufani.com
INKSTAINS ON THE EDGE OF LIGHT / BY HIND SHOUFANI
ISBN-13: 978-0-9845128-9-8
ISBN-10: 0-9845128-9-6
Library of Congress Control Number: 2010934555

Cover illustration and book design by Danielle KATTAR

Whole World Press does not have any control over and does not assume any
responsibility for author or third-party websites or their content.

DEDICATION PAGE

Raghida- for being the moon sister, fierce warrior of desert and inner oceans. Half of my mother's soul and guardian of her light. For your green eyes of Nazareth. I thank you and love you for being the best friend anyone could wish for in an aunt. And for the tie dye, the singing, the ginger candies, the freedom and our fragrant smoky evenings. And buckets of trail mix.

Ellen- for your unending grace, generosity with Yasmine, wild sense of humor and immense knowledge. I am proud. I thank you and love you for care, the best tiramisu ever, always listening to me and for finally coming around to buying me the most fabulous glitter gifts imaginable!

Janine- for strength and constant roaring laughter. For a home and a brilliant family. For delicious diet food and silent moments on your couch. For the gift of your wisdom, kindness and twinkly eyes. I thank you and love you for the "shilleh" in Amman/Dubai and for never leaving Yasmine's side. Or mine.

Mona- for the serene sorceress of my youth. For your home of small miracles, a garden of eternal treasure. For the stiff drinks when I needed them, the soft pauses in our tears, the nights spent in your haven. I thank you and love you for the tuna salad escapades, the cigarettes you let me smoke and spending your life quietly loving Yasmine.

Kathy- for that wide smile we all adore. For your Indian food, um Kulthoum on your wall, the stream of liberating books you brought to our life, for Christmas decorations handmade from your capable hands. I thank you and love you for letting me read for five days in bed, for advice and support and for always being there when Yasmine needed you.

Nothing I write could ever be enough.

Hind Shoufani

Hind Shoufani is a Palestinian filmmaker/writer, born as a refugee in Lebanon in 1978. She grew up in various cities in the Middle East and was a Fulbright scholar to NYU to obtain a Master of Fine Arts in Filmmaking from the Tisch School of the Arts. She currently works in the Middle East as a director/producer and writer. Winter she makes films for others, summer she makes films for herself. Throughout the year, she writes for everyone and no one.

She has no formal training in poetry. This is her second collection of poems, and if she has any say in the matter, it will not be her last. In 2007, she wrote a book of poems titled "More Light than Death Could Bear" published by xanadu*. She is also the founder of the Poeticians group, an elastic public reading entity where poets from all backgrounds perform spoken word and poetry in various Arab cities.

She is obsessed with glittery light but loves the dark. On her wish list is Leonard Cohen music, a free and secular Palestine, female rights and liberties and bonding with everyday warriors and freedom fighters all over the world. Blessed to still dance alone to addictive music, she loves to also update the Poeticians site and finds peace in looking for colorful shiny Hindu bindi jewels for her forehead.

She can be found at www.poeticians.com and, often, sipping coffee in cozy afternoon cafes of Beirut streets, or indulging in late-night Indian restaurants in Dubai.

Introduction
by Zena El Khalil

The first time I met Hind Shoufani, I understood that she carried a heavy burden.

Why else adorn oneself in a multitude of colors, a crystal that broke off and fell from the edge of a rainbow. Why else choose to wear fabrics that glide and flow; ready, ready to take flight at any given moment. Why else hide behind vibrant glitter; reflecting the sun, the moon… becoming one with light.

All this softness, all this… is a disguise.

Because at the root lies a fiery woman who has been burdened with a strong voice. Her swift pen etches us blistering songs, as she tries to find balance in the tumultuous whirlwinds around her. You see, Hind has been chosen to tell the story of her people and her world. Her place and her time. Even if she didn't want to. Even if she tried not to. She could not but do so.

Hind Shoufani, born a refugee, is burdened with the weight of being an educated and exceptional woman, from Palestine. She is burdened with the weight of being a storyteller of her generation. Stories of her homeland, slipping through her fingers. Her father, disheartened and shattered. Her mother, inspirational but deceased. Her lovers, flighty, unable to hold her down. Her present reality, torn and reconstructed over and over again. Like her heart. Like Beirut.

Her burden is her voice, strong and clear. Her ability to spill onto paper her rage, affection and her love. Her burden is her fervent desire to outplay death. To find life. To find a home. To find love. She is not afraid to sing. She is not afraid to question. Not afraid to question America. Not afraid to question Israel. Not even afraid to question present-day Palestine.

Hind Shoufani is burdened with the responsibility of being the memory box of her family. Collecting stories, ideas, history and life. Recording her father, recording her mother, keeping her sister at close hand. Finding Palestine, losing Palestine. She will not let go of her dead.

Her words are witness to histories from the world around her. The attacks on Mumbai. The stoning to death of a young Arab woman. Beirut when there was still Modca. The hazy deserts surrounding Dubai. The mystery and stagnation of Damascus. You will meet depressed and metaphysical Beiruti citizens. You will meet a tarot card reader. You will meet cancer. You will meet organs for sale in Israel. You will meet jasmine and Yasmine. The New York subway. You will meet men and women of the world who still know how to laugh and cry. There are revolutions and a guidebook to forgetfulness. You will meet genocide and religion and all that may not happen.

xanadu*, along with Whole World Press, is proud to be publishing Hind Shoufani's second book of poetry, standing firm to our belief that art and literature can make positive changes around the world. We are committed to supporting artists and writers, like Hind, who take personal initiatives to build bridges in order to make this world a truly beautiful place. Now, more than ever, her voice is needed. Her grace, tact, and often blunt declarations, will give readers a fresh insight on what it means to be young, beautiful, and courageous in the Middle East. Her sharp words never forgot how to forgive. Her heart writhing, never forgot how to love. She speaks for herself and for those who cannot. She speaks a language that is urgent. She speaks of the here and now. She is global. This nomad is at home in New York City, in Beirut, in Amman, in Damascus, in Jerusalem, in Dubai, anywhere.

And it is in this stratum that we can come to appreciate that Hind's burden is really Hind's gift.

Hind is here to stay. She will not let go of her dead. She will not let go of her dead.

Zena el Khalil
Beirut, 2010

Foreword
by Jean Said Makdissi

For Yasmine

The poems in this volume by Hind Shoufani are a powerful reminder that a new generation of Arab writers and poets have emerged from within the boundaries of local culture to embrace the world and enclose it in a new kind of language. Hind Shoufani's virtuosic use of English and its poetic practice is loaded with references to the modern Arab experience, and is thus neither pure English nor in any way Arabic-translated-into-English. Rather these poems are a wonderfully haunting bonding of a literary tradition with a political and cultural state of being as they touch each other and find transcendent expression in the self-conscious freedom of modernist techniques.

Though the poems are imbued with a quintessentially contemporary Arab sense of loss and frustration, with the sadness of personal nostalgic memory and regret, and with the sensuousness of physical love, they are loaded as well with merciless political perception, and a cosmopolitan view of the world based on the experiences of the poet in various places and cultures. This melange sometimes breeds a cynical humour, but often also a deep anger, and always a sensuality that translates perceptions into visions, scents, sounds and feelings. These elements together add a galloping rhythm and a sense of vitality and strength to the poems that offset the sadness: the poet never allows herself to drag us down into the boring and self-indulgent depths of self-pity and bathos.

Two recurring themes or images of loss dominate throughout, blending the personal and intimate with the public and political: the traumatic loss of her mother, Yasmine, at a young age, or, more accurately, the memory of her mother's dying and death, and the poet's inability or unwillingness to let the memory go of *"the tragedy /struck at the center of my family;"* and the loss of Palestine, which is, at least initially, directly tied up in the poet's mind with her father, the PLO activist and scholar Elias Shoufani. In fact, it is through his consciousness, which she seems instinctively not just to penetrate but to appropriate as well, taking it on herself as her own painful burden, that she, too young to have known it personally, vicariously experiences the loss of homeland and the bitterness of exile by re-telling the tale told to her. But even her love poems seem as much a celebration of the breaking of bonds, memory, and loss as of the direct experience of physical love.

The first chapter of the book, "Death," concentrates on Yasmine, her dying, her death and her memory, with which the poet struggles to come to terms. On the one hand she knows she should, she ought, she must, let her mother go, for both their sakes.

a stranger tells me
it hurts the dead
it saddens them to stay
trapped in a noose of our shackles

Over and over in the first poem she writes of the necessity of "letting go": The stranger, reading tarot cards, tells her

stories that preach
to release,
to let go of the intimate dead
enter the forgetfulness of sobriety and the
march on of sunlit hours

The dead and dying mother is the prisoner of the poet's memory; she is locked in it, shackled to her daughter's pain, as the daughter is shackled to the mother's. Yasmine's physical degradation and suffering is thus prolonged in the memory, though in fact death had mercifully released her, let her go, years before.

Though she tries, the poet will not let go; she is terrified of losing the loss, of forgetting the painful memories to which she clings:

this fragile
tenuous grasp i hold
lingers
safeguarded are those finite
breaths we inhaled of you
but one must now
find a dumpsite for the dead to rest

The word "dumpsite," suggesting that to overcome a memory is to transform it into rubbish, a putrefied, rotten, smelly thing to be discarded without further thought, betrays the guilt she would feel if she should let it go, abandon the beauty of her attachment to her mother's being, which now exists only in her mind. In any case, no matter how hard she tries, she cannot let go:

how do i let that go
how do i free her from being in me
from being so in
how to accept how she's now too far away

The memory is too powerful, the loss felt anew every day:

the cursed sunlight, another enemy
unvanquished
and she is never there
i remember
the sunlight
the day starts
she is never there
always, reminders, fact of her loss
i awake and
she will never be there

This, the poet says bitterly to the tarot card reader who tells her she must let go, "*is not math or science or literary opportunity . . . and romantic tragedy:*"

This is your mother, sick in a bed,
haggard,
Life stolen seconds endless till she is
a corpse, bled out

Indeed, it is more the dying, than the living Yasmine that her daughter cannot forget. Only occasionally do we get a hint of the live, vibrant mother:

that softness in her grass eyes
that wind in motion in her hair

The poem ends with a refusal to release the memory, herself, and her mother from their mutually entangling embrace:

i will not let go of my dead
i will not let go of my dead

A second shorter poem continues the theme, but is less assuring of the steadfastness of memory. "I Forget", which, we are reminded with a raw jab, is "for Yasmine, whom it's always for." Here the images that the poet, afraid of losing them, captures and sets down in her powerful words, include glimpses of the living Yasmine, but they are always supplanted by the dying one. Tormented with fear and guilt, she asks:

What happens if I can no
Longer conjure your face
. . .
the changes in your space
from laughter
to hospital beds in silence
. . .
what if i forget the color of the pajamas
the hospital gave us
you were not reduced to anyone as a number
yet walking proved too difficult
your belly a vegetable
dry rotting cruel
your mind adrift in the leaving of us
beloved us

But the promise made to the dying that one will never forget, always remember, is betrayed by *"time.*

. . a cruel jester" and is becoming harder to keep. The poem ends with the plaintive lament:

if only it could be easy
if only you had stayed with us, mother

If the poems about her mother focus on "the intimate dead," the diseased body and its irrevocable descent to death and oblivion, the first poem to her father, "Cello Talk," which is "For Elias Shoufani, who is incomparable," uses many of the same intimate details of physical decline, as well as mental, but expands outwards, away from the excruciating private and into the equally excruciating public and political sphere. Her father is the one who knew, and passed on to her, the story of loss and betrayal that is the Palestinian experience: It is he who *"made falastine for me a place of magic/and tenderness/and steadfastness."* His memories and experience become hers:

a home
stolen
land stolen
pets stolen
your father's funeral
stolen
the last goodbye of your mother
stolen
my teenage angst
stolen
my mother's future expectant
stolen
passports money time thought energy peace solidarity family

sisters
brothers
nieces
bicycles and vine leaves
uncle Jamil's cucumbers at dawn
stolen
and here you are, hands empty, old
and here you are,
leaving me
and even a possible death in peace,
stolen

Her father has bequeathed to her

everyday wisdom and pent up fury
an infallible sense of justice
an Arab dream soaring above your weakened nerves

The many references to his physical decline --"blood seeping from your parts/private / and not;" " the flesh you inhabited betraying you;" "your flaccid hands/ swollen ankles on your frame so heavy;" "silver streaks in thick curly hair" -- are achingly tender, and she is preparing to mourn him:

my fingers yelping on this page to mourn you
to prepare my life to your absence
to give up the ties that breathed me
the hands that molded
the eyes that sheltered
and as you sink legs first into the quicksand of aging
as you linger and linger at the door of eternal silence
I am on the war march to scream out chants to your
  kindness. . . .

But it is clear that she is equally, if not more, moved by the demise of his early promise, the irrepressible fighter for justice in Palestine who has been ignored, and who has failed:

where have your childhoods' far
fetching dreams gone? where have your brown
arms clutching weapons, paper, ink,
my youth, gone?
leaving me with stories, breathless.

His "hawk eyes"

. . . have vultured the betrayal of nations
who did not listen to you
who did not care
cloaks of rhetoric hid their deception
and you spent a lifetime seeking their salvation
your own murdered nights a price
we all found high, except you. . .

He had given up the idea of a normal family life, and *"the entitlement you were owed of greatness/ of the possibility of what they call/happiness"* and, unlearning *"the chitchat of serene humanity"* by taking up *"the jagged edges of politics"* left his family wondering how to comfort him by saying *"anything/, something/ in the face of this sadness/we call falastine."*

The power of this poem—and the others on the poet's complex relationship with Palestine in the third chapter, entitled "Home" -- lies in her ability to capture in personal mode the essence of the endless losses, violence, disappointments, and humiliations that make up the modern history of this place, and its victims, as well as the indelible thought of Palestine itself as it is steadfastly kept alive by its people, who, like her, will not give it up. She does this by concentrating on a language of negative imagery and diction rapped out sometimes at a hurtling pace which recalls the explosions and gun-fire of the 60-odd year conflict,

. . . . they
hid your unlawful
ungodly captivity
the bloodshed
shed hourly
on your scene of nativity

but also sometimes at a gentler, softer pace which calls up the rhythms of dreams and of laments:

they told me when i could open my eyes
that you were full of wonder
men women lived as angels under your trees
they told me fairy tales of princes that kneeled
mad with love
on their knees
they told me you were bountiful

She opens the first poem of "Home" with a line of unconventional frankness, which expresses the weary thought that no doubt has crossed many a Palestinian mind:

i am so tired of you palestine

This line is repeated throughout the poem, and acts as a chorus of rejection and almost renunciation: those who have for several generations carried the burden of Palestine, with its endless litany of loss, deprivation, dispossession, and violent persecution, as well as the betrayal, hypocrisy and lies of local and international leaders, are now weary:

i am so tired of living with you
of your life inside me
invisibly
the articles of your wardrobe
replete with beads of suffering
every morning you dress me with terror
you feed me lunacy
and massacres
and tragedy

In the end, however, the poet cannot give up her attachment to Palestine, and rather takes it on as her own experience. As the long poem progresses, and she wrestles with the issue, the name of Palestine undergoes a silent, but cunning, transformation from its English, or foreign, name to its Arabic, and more authentic one, *falastine*. At first the poet has a perception of the place as a geographic or historic entity whose problems, from which she wishes to distance herself, have dragged her down to the depths of despair. As she thinks about it, however, she gradually moves away from this position, and appropriates the direct experience of Palestine, and becomes aware that she is organically attached to it. From her standing in this new place emerges her adoption of the Arabic name. The poem ends as it began, with an articulation of intense fatigue, but now with affirmation and reclamation, inevitably, organically, replacing renunciation and rejection:

*i am so tired ya falasteen,
i am tired of loving you
and hating you
and loving you
fundamentally
intrinsically
instinctively
eternally*

The usual images of heroic armed resistance, with fighters winning military successes, is absent from these poems on Palestine. And while the heroic steadfastness and refusal of its people to surrender to a superior force-- a major theme of modern Palestinian consciousness -- is often implicitly lauded, it is rather the essential injustice, the inhumanity, the militarization, the suffering of the people, that she expresses, over and over again, as well as the stubborn hanging on, almost against their will, of individual Palestinians, like the poet herself, which is celebrated here.

It is difficult without endless quotation to summarize, or even to hint at, the power of the poet's expression of attachment, however reluctant, to the cause. In successive poems --"Conversations/Inebriations/ Demonstrations," "To the tens of thousands in the streets, protesting, in my heart" (dated January, 2009, during the massive Israeli assault on Gaza), "Organs on sale for Israel," (also dated January, 2009) and many others -- Hind Shoufani expresses sorrow, outrage, indignation, nostalgia in a painful series of images, some metaphoric, many naturalistic, all strikingly direct and moving.

The theme of the second chapter of this book, entitled "Life," is writing, and specifically writing poetry, and consists of a series of poems dedicated to various people in the poet's life. One after another, the poet sings, snarls, declaims, announces, denounces the human experience, and the writing of it. Again the poet's basic humanity comes to the defence of the suffering, the constant, the just, the loving, the faithful – the qualities of humanity – that she constantly admires. The first poem, dedicated to the poet, writer and civil rights activist June Jordan who, like Yasmine, died of cancer, and who wrote a memoir of her own illness which, echoed by Hind, painfully recalls Yasmine's suffering; the descriptions of the diseased body mutilated by successive surgeries is startlingly realistic, startlingly visual and sensory, so that one can see and feel the wounds, smell the body, be there by the bedside, with the patient and her nurses. But in the end it is with the black poet's free spirit, more than her wounded body, that Hind Shoufani identifies, and the poem ends thus:

and my heart is burdened
but, like yours
it's free
it's free

One of the most powerful poems is entitled "for the record" and is dedicated to "my students who cared about their world." Dated 2008 in Beirut, it re-creates the images in a documentary film on the stoning of a young woman. The poem is full of graphic descriptions of the inhuman process:

Thud Thud Thud
went the stone brick, into her
temples, cheeks, nose splintered, eyes sunk in
into her future,

The major companion theme is the cruelty of the men who are stoning the young woman, of her family that has abandoned her to this horrible fate, and the social system that allows this sort of thing. In the end, as the girl's life is pounded out of her broken body, the words of the killers degenerate into American street vernacular, recalling the worst sort of TV or movie representations of such acts, and thus suggesting the universality of violence against women. But it also suggests that we, who are reading the poem and through it watching the film, are mere passive spectators to the horrors of our world. We watch, but we do not stop the torments of the suffering.

The poem ends with the imagined words of the killers, who transform their own apparent terror at the evil they have accomplished into a triumphant declaration of success in the meanest possible way:

we got her good man,
it took fourteen of us, three bricks,
and some heavy boots,
we got her, we didn't even have to use the sticks.
Fucking whore, little cunt thought she would split

with him, we got her, little shithead
aint moving
another
fucking
inch.

The last chapter of the book, entitled "Lust," is a series of love poems. Through the words of the poet one feels the sensuality of the hot humid nights of love-making, principally it seems in Beirut. As usual, however, the poet transcends mere flesh, and in this case, sexuality, and rises to the same moral and almost spiritual values she has proclaimed throughout the book. Along with the intense and very explicit descriptions of the physical encounters, friendship, companionship, shared human principles, meetings of minds – all these become the true object of her expression. But again the poems are imbued with farewells, renunciations, separations. For this poet, pure sexuality, pure physical experience, is never enough: today and now are never enough. The past is always beckoning, a severe judge of actions, thoughts, words.

I give you up
lover
you could not know me
we make gravity in different planets
the collision of your lips on mine
brutal sexy
infrequent and alight with electricity
is but passing spark
is sheer fantasy
is delicacy
temporary

If she states here that what she wants out of life and love is beyond the immediate and the physical, she ends her collection with a poem that recognizes that her demand is too great for the real world. The poem, entitled "The Rules," is dedicated to "all my lovely single girlfriends," and is a sermon on the theme "never love a man who. . ." is selfish and self-centred, and who, worst of all, does not love back to the same degree that he is loved.

The poem opens with

Never love a man who has not called to
anxiously check whether you did get sick and could possibly be in bed
retching your inner guts while making excuses for
his busy self, traveling.

With its constant repetition of the chorus line *"never love a man who...."* it becomes vaguely reminiscent of Rudyard Kipling's poem "If," but, unlike "If," that same repetition grants it a degree of much needed humour. One can almost see a group of young women gathered to hear their friend's wise admonitions, and laughing in recognition of the familiar snubs that only men can render, and only women put up with.

The poem ends, however, on a more serious note:

never,
never have his children,
never let go of your private
oceans and jungles and deserts to chase his name,
and never,

never ever I say,
never admit that this too is a poem for him.

Like all the other poems in this volume the emphasis is on fidelity, love, the reciprocal bonds of a shared and equal humanity.

A last word about these poems: there is no question that they could not have been written except by a woman. These are not feminist poems in the narrow sense of the word: they do not, except on occasion, make explicit social demands of the reader. But they are deeply feminist in the highest, widest and most important sense of the word. Their significance lies in the fact that they investigate, proclaim, declaim, sometimes mourn and deplore, but always *sing,* the female consciousness, which is at the heart of the world.

CHAPTER ONE
DEATH

DEATH CARD DEALER, TAROT READER, I CRY

For Zena and Maral, who never forget to love.
Beirut, 06/2008

A stranger tells me
kindly
unfolding cards only she deconstructs
i must let you go

one must not keep captive her dead

this fragile
tenuous grasp i hold
lingers
safeguarded are those finite
breaths we inhaled of you
but one must now
find a dumpsite for the dead to rest

she tells me it's for the best

meanwhile
in an act meant as mercy
compassion
humility, there are those who trust

those who believe, those who assure the
struggling rest of us
stuck in a spiritual mess, they confirm
and attest
that they are buried within us those dead
we exalted and held and smiled for
they are
wrapped within us in energy
transformed mute
a sensation of not being alone in the quiet
　　　night
they are with us
dreams wet with liquid you seep when you see
　　　them
and on awaking
the damn echoes
in the night
wild unseen out of reach
out of bounds aloft
a distant flight
and i awake
the cursed sunlight, another enemy
unvanquished
and she is never there
i remember
the sunlight
the day starts

DEATH

she is never there
always, reminders, fact of her loss
i awake and
she will never be there

my aunt tells me over and over
of whispered calls that she hears
alone
on a restless night
my aunt who held and held
on tight
my aunt is who is full of light
hope has flourished
she has ended her fight
my aunt has found her own way

a stranger collects the cards
reads to me ancient images i decipher not
tales of life clenched on to death spread among
    the tragedy
struck at the center of my family
stories afraid ablaze in hurt alight
at the start of my need
that softness in her grass eyes
that wind in motion in her hair
stories that preach

DEATH

to release,
to let go of the intimate dead
enter the forgetfulness of sobriety and the
march on of sunlit hours
i bear i dread
the welcomed apathy of the receding memory
do it she says
i cannot do it   it does not become me
i am lost in lanes of your absence
and alleyways of words you have bequeathed
    me
words to reach out
to you and godless
i pray

a stranger tells me
it hurts the dead
it saddens them to stay
trapped in a noose of our shackles
those memories we term love
on this determined tormented state
named earth
clumsy we are in our thoughts
un-understood
by them
those who are free who are in places i cannot
    believe

are even real
stuck i remain in those tongues of clay

where do they go these dead we must leave
where are your hands now
how do you keep your smile on
how do you float and think and breathe
what happened to those lips you kissed us
    with
where are those limbs you shook the dust of
    sadness with
where are your fingertips baking and kneading
    and shriveling and clenched
and open
and raw and sometimes around me and
    sometimes
close enough within
where are your sighs
and bursts of songs
and a million books to teach me everything
you could not say in the span
of a lifetime
taken in by hurt and disease and how do i
    forgive their
god this sin, i who does not believe
how do i let that go
how do i free her from being in me

from being so in
how to accept how she's now too far away

the dead are their own existence

i await the days those words can sink in
strangers hand me tissues
traces of mourning you stain my face
in permanent black ink
for repeated it is the savagery of grief
even bearing witness to
that kindness in her tarot reading
eyes black deep impenetrable
she understood
everyone had
has will have and forever will gather
a love for a dead other
but one must stop weeping she says

one must let go of the dead

stand still
do not fall apart by naked will
when confronted by wisps of their life
hurtled at you in hour after unexpected hour
the explosion universal

of my interior
the tears i can keep sprouting for you as flowers
over and over again given to you for time immortal
how does
how does one let go of the dead
i who do not believe
still feel her energy
she feels
my enlightened friends
and lovers
and strangers who have kept me company
who
claim claim away
claim a salvation of belief in transference
and energy and the cycle of everything that is flowing
everything tumbles into one
becomes the essence of what's in me
in our inner lives we are all in harmony
in a grand scheme i must faithfully perceive
in this cosmic part i play
they say
that we are with each other, whether we touch our hands to your
shoulder and chest and elbow and lips

or not, whether we falter in our hopes
and people disappear in our thoughts,
they wither
we are all still together, and she is here, you
    just can't see her
and i,
i want to see her
i want her to be here
i want her to stay

how do we erase the sight of the dead
the taste of our taken dead
the sound they trickled into our arms
the hammered wails your absence chants in
    my head
this empty bed
the way your pictures startle me and
i eventually have started to speak them
in an exercise of sheer futility that nonetheless
plagues me and shackles me
and allows me some affinity with you
some return of you to mend the ache
of my family
my sanity
astray

it is not enough

DEATH

never enough
this salvation in belief they harp out at me
it is not
how does one let go of the dead
this is not math nor science nor literary opportunity
for poetry and divine comedy
and romantic tragedy
this is your mother, sick in a bed,
haggard,
life stolen seconds endless till she is
a corpse, bled out
by forces not familiar
forces i understand not
and cannot conquer
forces i, warrior i, cannot keep at bay
and how i long to stop time
stop this stranger
from having to convince me one
must let the anger
and the memory of her inner
laughter
go
further
one must not choke the dead no matter how we
need to have her

we must let her get away

despite all those cards she opened
stories of promised
love and children i am to create,
that demon of fate
tarnished with hate has imbued me with
a void,
a hole in a space which she had shaped
and i don't see how all the theories
or stories told
all the magic books i hold,
even all the poems still untold,
the lies i was fed with, bought and sold by
strangers and i, always
trying to be kind
to the bereaved
all those tales they weaved
and
cards opened in faith and humility,
can ever cease can ever diminish can ever change
my certainty of mourning
always
my words a dirge for eternity
for

DEATH

how does one let go of the dead?

a stranger tells me it's for the best,
help send off the contented dead
to their death
and if only i knew what that is, and i
i who do
not
believe
i selfish
i devoured by love and tears
shed
and by this knot i cannot sever
i want to keep her with me forever and ever
and ever

i will not let go of my dead
i will not let go of my dead

I FORGET

For Yasmine, whom it's always for.
Beirut, 04/2008

what happens if i can no
longer conjure your face
if i cannot one day trace
the outline of your movements
to picture the grace
with which you stumbled through death the
loss of familiar smells to you
the changes in your space
from laughter
to hospital beds in silence
anguish a new game you taught us
what if i forget the color of the pajamas
the hospital gave us
you were not reduced to anyone as a number
yet walking proved too difficult
your belly a vegetable
dry rotting cruel
your mind adrift in the leaving of us
beloved us

and what happens if i lose
your lines and curves

and edges of color

this poem is violence and mostly words unsaid
i did not write for you then
but i memorized the three important lines
one must repeat to the dying
we love them
we will always remember them
they are in our hearts
we love them
we will always remember them
they are in our minds

you think this is absolute truth
they die

but you and i discover
time is a cruel jester
time, you fucker
give me back my memories
give me back my mother
i dare not imagine what would happen
if i can remember
her energy
her tragedy
no longer

DEATH

if only it could be easy
if only you had stayed with us, mother

CELLO TALK

For Elias Shoufani, who is incomparable.
Beirut, 10/2007

this time
the cellos have ushered in the dirge
of your announced death
in a trance
in Beirut
moaning of delicate strings bespoke of your
    absence
while you breathed yet
hours away
blood seeping from your parts
private
and not
and i, entranced by music and solitude
precious in Beirut
transported my presence to your vision
i left the shell of this dazzle in my house
to move unsupported
in realms witnessing your decline
your fall from fame
the flesh you inhabited betraying you
after all this time spent, after all this age
seconds zing

sparks of your genius trudge on
and you will bequeath me
everyday wisdom and pent up fury
an infallible sense of justice
an Arab dream soaring above your weakened nerves
your flaccid hands
swollen ankles on your frame so heavy
as you clenched teeth and maintained your fist quiet
at the death around us mounting
falastine
beyroot
yasmeen
where have your childhoods' far
fetching dreams gone? where have your brown
arms clutching weapons, paper, ink,
my youth, gone?
leaving me with stories, breathless

silver streaks in thick curly hair
hawk eyes have vultured the betrayal of nations
who did not listen to you
who did not care
cloaks of rhetoric hid their deception
and you spent a lifetime seeking their salvation

your own murdered nights a price
we all found high, except you, you who knew
a home
stolen
land stolen
pets stolen
your father's funeral
stolen
the last goodbye of your mother
stolen
my teenage angst
stolen
my mother's future expectant
stolen
passports money time thought energy peace
    solidarity family
sisters
brothers
nieces
bicycles and vine leaves
uncle Jamil's cucumbers at dawn
stolen
and here you are, hands empty, old
and here you are,
leaving me
and even a possible death in peace,

stolen

she creeps her head in again
my foe of clear nights and rushed embraces
my specter of loss looming in traces
subtle
yet permanently
painting remembered imagery of cold lips
closed eyelids
frigid hips
and the lack of your voice echoing love,
lost mother

and here you are father ignoring her ghost
vibrating your
house corners
you are looking headlong into the abyss
while we twist and turn in a furnace
our hands tied
our tongues occupied with drivel
our hearts bursting with madness
my fingers yelping on this page to mourn you
to prepare my life to your absence
to give up the ties that breathed me
the hands that molded
the eyes that sheltered

and as you sink legs first into the quicksand of aging

as you linger and linger at the door of eternal silence

i am on the war march to scream out chants to your kindness

to your sacrifices

the efforts given away of your flesh bone hair and eyes

your calmness

the way you made falastine for me a place of magic

and tenderness

and steadfastness

i am left with words echoing your hardness

the willpower you donned as armor

to keep able to shut out the drabness

of our third world weakness

Beirut Gaza Damascus

and you ventured your spirit unvalued

you gave away the promised land of milk and honey

you threw away the stillness of life in America

and the entitlement you were owed of greatness

of the possibility of what they call

happiness

and instead you started a path

to mountains blaring trumpets of despair
war zones
bad shoes
hasty midnight dinners in camps unwashed
un centered
you unlearnt the chitchat of serene humanity
and accustomed yourself to the jagged edges
    of politics
heroics
dying on mine filled lands
days stolen by an enemy only you could
    properly see
while we all stumbled around you aching
wondering thinking yearning for a way
to say
anything
something
in the face of this sadness
we call falastine

cellos vibrate
the drone of this
date unknown, not captured to paper,
stone, death certificates
hopeless dreams
lack of gleam
lack of breath giving us steam

DEATH

and yet i listen for they call gently, clearly
softly they say to me
it's time
time to let go of the present
the sorrow born of your history father
time to allow you gently to forgo this life
we the young ones hold dear
this life you can stand no longer
this anger rising tides in you
the loss of homeland now a certainty
the lack of heroes
the lack of possibility

i learn to say goodbye with every hello we share
i learn to clench my pumping heart
to still my grinding teeth
to accept that i am not called upon
that you alone will be able to follow the siren song
of the cellos that commit you
to a new home,
i wander off to a land of dreams
while my fingers consign the ashes of your fire
and earth and flesh and water
to words

52   for now
      we still breathe

ONE ZERO

For Nuya, who doesn't need to speak in words.
Beirut, 28/12/2007

my hands propel themselves
tears have forced the fingers to seek asylum
i do not want to write

ten years since i last saw your eyes close
silent trickles
moisture
i knew not where your private thoughts were
your heart beat in white sheets
toes restless,
beeping screens
hushed whispers
telling me you can still hear us

we still played music for you then
and i do not want to write

i lose the letters on my way here
palms dry neck arched back stiff
gut clenched in fear
hate too at the ten years gone by
since your coffin was open

eyes closed
and in mine tear after tear after tear
of anger
i do not want to write

yet the fingers are pushed forward
by winds that howl
and wail
and sneer
gusts of your absence hurtle me
whispers only i can hear

and i do not want to write
it has been ten years

i would
give up all the sentences ever possible
throw away another ten hard years
sacrifice the solace of memory
if only
i could have you back for one more day
one more stolen moment
to say
we love you

i do not want to write tonight

DEATH

and you,
mother
my beautiful mother

you are not here

Y AND Z

For my beloved and missed Teta Z.
Beirut, 11/2007

how do i know when it
is over, this seeping
river of seething
leaking
into moments unexpected
uninvited, rested
i had sat and this cigarette i lit
warned not
of a thought rushing heedless
to remind
so needless
to further bind my misery
entwined i am with the disbelief rampant
of the loss of only you
sketched
etched
your absence becoming
concrete of my flesh
and
how do i explode free?
i do not know how to perceive
a way out

DEATH

a way to not
stay in an endless state
of grieve
the emptiness i fill not
the heat i cool not
the tears i do not reprieve
let me let go
just let me let go
let me believe
let me relieve
please tell me
please
help me
let me stop this
let me rest
in the eternal abyss of letting you slip through
my crooked wretched fingers
memory after memory warped
squeezed
through this unyielding sieve

NEWSCAST

Dubai, 03/2009

everyday
the news that you strapped this death to your chest and
bestowed it on our people
in the name of Allah, whom
you loved,
whom you loved more than our people, whom you worshipped more
than love, whom you knew better than the
rest of us
heathens

everyday
you wrapped that end to your chest
and took limbs
eyes
hands
feet with you to the unknown places destined
soon
far too soon for the children
running in sewers of tears
now desolate
hushing their voices that pleaded

palm trees, desperate.

Baghdad
Gaza
Kabul
cities of murder, not suicide cities of heresy
cities of genocide
cities of longing for the god you served
to come wash away this soil of blood
to clean away your
misery to wipe away this apathy to weed out
    this pathology
this atrocity you call
salvation,
this war you want you think you win
these spoils of flesh you think you gain
the demise of yet another proud Arab nation

i pull my lover to my chest, i stroke his dark
    skin, gentle
i let my fingers heal all the unspoken
depths
i let my lips like spring rain
blossom the silence between us eternal, i send
    skin to
harvest this energy, to
throw out into the wind the fervent kisses we

devour
i make sure my lullaby cleanses away any shadow of ache
any stain

you take dynamite
metal
wires
timers
tnt
anything that is crafted carefully
to reduce a market a church a school a mosque a funeral procession
with your fire
your shrapnel of flesh
in the name of all that's holy
in the name of all that is ignored, defeated, scared and tired,
and i wonder if you knew
what you were killing, or who, or why
or what for, again
and again
shia
sunni
catholic
jewish
kurdi

DEATH

salafist
wahhabi
nazi

you tire me. you don't inspire me. you fill me
    to the
brim with searing
Arab shame

i close my eyes
listen to the constant breath of my lover's life,
that force in him steady
that strength unchecked, unmasked,
    unearthed for my beauty
and as the dreams of
nights in safety dispel yet another
newscast of strife,
i wish
i wish
i pray you were a child i could hold, a hand
i could guide, a memory i could change,
an infant i could rush to in the solitude of the
    night and
offer that one gift which would make all
the difference, that would set your future right,
that one word that would guarantee a
path to non-violence

a sentence
a poem
a kiss to render you silent, a book i would be
for you to send you
knowledge, and my god of patience,
my god of tolerance,
my god of benevolent kindness
how i wish how i wish we could unstrap that sadness
from your chest
and tell you how exquisite you can be
naked
how merciful our god can be,
how human we can be
if we only spoke
if we only held
if we only accepted
instead of murdered
a hand i would extend to you, to walk that river of calm you need you
lost, to be that one ebbing force making
the universe unfold in you
in reverent peace
in our warmth
teaching
what is sacred

what is sacred
is
us

GUIDEBOOK TO FORGETFULNESS

Dubai, 02/2009

it is ugly
the sudden nature of grief, smirking at
months of jaunting in daily spheres oblivious
to what you thought to be
forgotten
or not needed as remembrance
that one smile that had to be
photographed from your youth
slides adjacent to this present hole in my
    center
a colorless imprint on that stain of loss
permanently stamped on this
grand theft of
only you
how the wisdom of the earth confounds
deludes into ever thinking
of reconciling this absence
this malice
with solace
you shadow days in the silence of any given
    night
and i

have
spent
years
without you, shoved on by grief immense,
by grief antagonistic, by grief
intolerant
by grief unmoved by pleas
by grief never benevolent
i have spent years dancing
to private dirges,
face aging,
radiant above
an undercurrent of hate rotten,
a torrent, sometimes merely a semblance of
this small stream, this steady flow,
constant drainage it is this
cesspool of tears stored out of the sight of others
an army of mourning marching at the gates
of this hell i harbor
in this state of hate,
and i miss you,
and i miss you,
and i have spent years
asking no one
all the possible

66　　questions
looking for the manual, the method, the instructions.

Countdown

Beirut, 01/2009

The day that you left me, i noticed three
new grey hairs
peeking out of the red
army once marching
now quavering on curly pugnacious trails
afraid of the battle
unwon
but i noticed
fault lines appeared on edges of that snow
    horizon
between my temple and the sight of you, deep
furrows in that desert between
your face and my smile of you
the tips of my fingers could never get warm
    enough
the bounce in my knees slid heavy, nails
    fractured
at the first collision
with matter, and flesh dimpled in toxins,
    gravity a
murderer
relentless
the day that you left me, i dismantled all the
    music boxes

a dirge eternal fluttering by my ears
cold, on the lookout for your voice
a scar on my thigh grew tremulous, but remained
steadfast digging further into the cracks
of my river like veins, all my
splintering surface
unraveled
the day that you left me, i slept because i took a pill
and could not distinguish since then whether i woke up
and cities have burned, and entire families wiped out
in the space it takes to
remember you
buoyant
my stomach pulsing with the sight of you
my eyesight gorging, rampant, breathless. Beirut has
put on her mourning suit, again, ageless,
starched, ready at hand that costume, to welcome
war, and its religious trumpets. Damascus has slid into
distance, and refused to resurrect her martyrs, and
Amman has built concrete

DEATH

trenches around the voices of all of us,
new cities burned marks indelible on my
   carcass. And the people
have come
and the people have gone, and my arms have
   opened and
closed, and i have been alone in the dawn,
and i have been together in nights, entwined,
   endless. But the day
that you left me,
death fractured itself, cracked and went with
   you
and the other half, that vital section,
has crept slowly over the expanses of love
   witnessed
and now makes a home here
regardless of how hard i fought, regardless.
   The day
that you left me, i started a path towards
you, beyond the
light, behind my eyes,
following you,
frantic
restless. The day that you left me, i befriended
the demise of all the years to come
now
senseless.

FAITH

For the victims of the Mumbai terrorist attacks.
Abu Dhabi, 27/11/2008

your belief in your god of holy damnation
and sexist mythology
your god of people chosen
and preferable ideology
your god who condones your murder of my sisters
and my brothers who care not for your laws and rigid structures that
want to cage my innate humanity
your belief in your god who tells you
it is duty to rip the bellies of women
pregnant with life, with beauty,
and it is victory to twist
the bodies of your current enemy into
charred remains of masculinity, and it is prayer
to bring down buildings
toppled on those oblivious to your rancor
your anger
your belief in this god you profess
to follow has enabled
you to set our watches daily to the news of your holy

crusades of atrocity
your scripture based views
every day
the same banality
fires, explosions, gunmen cowards masked and children blasted in
open spaces, lives but specks of dust
abused
in your frenzied lust
to please this god you blindly trust
will honor your war unjust with martyrdom
that you must
pursue for if you
kill as many sinful fucks as you can
as many whores as you can
as many infidels as you can
exterminate all the ones with the wrong color
eyes, and the wrong color hair
the wrong accent or birthplace, or skin too dark
or skin too fair
the ones with the wrong gender
for yes, your belief is just
your belief is crucial to your heavens above
and the end justifies all your means
and what this means
is your desires reign supreme, you, you who knows best,

you who believe in the god that is best,
and us,
the rest who dare disagree are now but limbs
a torn belly, bleeding eye sockets and
slashed throats that won't ever
speak again of your
horror on UK telly
we are but breasts to be cut open
we are but feet to fling into dust
we are brain matter and finger tips and matted hair
and you don't have to care
for your god is right
your god is there for you
and vengeance on all sinners is all you have to swear

well
i swear
by the god i believe in
which is not your god, nor theirs, nor here in this land, nor up there
this god i feel in my center so bare
this god who tells me to dare
be strong
this god will forgive me this desire to plunge my hand

DEATH

and tear out that
rotten gut you wear for show, that gut that works no longer, and to
stomp out
your hatred into silence, to gnash out
all that anger in your eyes
unfair
your voice anguished with misguided despair

and my god will forgive me this murder

to make sure the earth
remains motherly
remains there
for those of us who hold on for another yearly daily hourly
moment of freedom
to say
i am there for you peaceful brother
i am there for you peaceful sister
no matter what color
what shape
what happiness you believe in, i am
there
no heaven needed to encourage me no hell needed to frighten me no holy fury required to inspire me

DEATH

my love is free and open and solitary
i am there already for you
i am there
i am there

SOMETIMES

For Jameel Shoufani, another Palestinian uncle I did not get to know.
Beirut, 04/2008

it is unbearable this life
unlivable
this death

youngsters flash eyes out anxious
startled
legs swoop out of nests and soar in uncertainty
but yet in motion
universities await, and lovers on grass that's wet and new
birth pangs
Condy Rice with her gross smile
the Middle East peace process
in pieces
lives cheap
and the rush to a doctor mid night to save a life
death awaits in small events of inconsequence
i see it
my cousin
my sister
my best friend
my imaginary brother

awaiting you every morn are
dates to break, food to avoid, and bellies churning
with the daily bread
given not bought
destiny a notion pleasant to many
the careless many
yet they go these young ones they go

all the way to the door of my uncle's death bed

he died in my hometown tonight
i did not know him
he was a blue-eyed ghost in my father's silences
he was the lingering scent of a Galilee garden before anyone awoke
i did not know him
i am of him
and he is of me
we share name family dna and a mean temper
i did not love him
i did not know to love him
but i commit to eternal memory the
one summer i walked his pathways
he shuffled towards me
in an earth drenched language

i understood little
he gestured gruffly
to offer me cucumbers
he had woken at dawn to gather for me
his missing niece
the missing piece in this family of aged love
and barbed wire and
solid old olive trees
and then, years later away again,
my uncle died in pain. my father has not seen him in thirty some years.

i am thirty now
Israel still rules me
yet death is far still
tucked in my cells that shiver denial
but ache is closer
ache is closer still
ache makes a home here
and my father, oh my father, i will not tell you of this death tonight
you sleep
Palestine a lost dream
lost family you mourned is now steeped in more loss
i will not tell you tonight for you to
turn

and toss
alone again tonight

i will not tell my luminous sister
who may not remember my uncle's one
    gesture of love
she may not have eaten those cucumbers
but she lives her own truth with him
in her own refugee way
me
me, i was eighteen and
Yasmine was fading
childhood receding
and my uncle brought me offering from his soil
i could then see him, on this fragrant walk he
    took
the vine leaves pregnant
picking vegetables
i can see his heart still shattered
beating
they told me he loved a woman once
in another century
they told me he lost a woman once
and never replaced her
my bachelor uncle
died tonight

yet the limbs march on

weddings, birthday cakes, the lesson plan for tomorrow
vitamin supplements one must not forget
the sun rages on
it is unbearable this life
mixing death in her folds
intricate

my uncle died in pain tonight
i did not know to love

yet this is for him
an etching of eternal memory
a story on paper to make a tombstone
a smile at his blue eyes peeking from other realms

and perhaps acceptance
that my eyes shall blossom in the morn
and his will not
perhaps a surrender
to forgo resistance
and believe
perhaps he really is at peace
and it is i

DEATH

only i left with my own name
my own turn

it is unbearable this life
sometimes

Y, THANK YOU FOR THE VISITS

Dubai, 4/11/2009

I call on you when the nights are heavy, when
    the head lolls
on hard pillows of slumber lost, when the
    mind
astray
cannot shut out the darkness of day, when the
joints ache to protest this lack of repose,
when my lover soundly drifts off to planets
    without me,
and I am here,
body humming with negative energy to quell
    this silence,
when the tumbling thoughts turn despair into
tears and back into anguish,
returning to a place of nonsense, a land of
suspension between planes
unspoken, the veins drum with absence, and I
    am
buzzed, with longing, with hurt, with abandon,
I call on you, I repeat a mantra to come
bring the calm, to come
appease the limbs,
to come brush the skin with ease,
to come close the veil behind the eyes that

wont dream,
to come hold hands, to hold feet, to hold waists,
to hold my fears in the arms of your smile,
to say, sleep, to say, I can still be here,
I call for you when the world has me locked in battle,
knee deep in violence,
and remembrance. I call on you, a repeated prayer that numbs
the jitters, that is a balm for spirit restless,
that is a tonic for lips parched, for chest heavy, for stomach nauseous.
I call on you and it does not matter that you have left me,
for ten years of theft and injustice,
I can hear the mute words you sing,
I can feel the heat invading pores breathless,
I can sleep to the image of your speech, behind these eyes searching
for a dream to perhaps see you without the knowledge
of this earth,
cruel, malevolent, heartless.
I call on you when there is nothing left of this world.
I call on you when the earth is as small as the distance

between your name and my voice inner,

when the night brings me messages from realms you roam,

when the memory of you is a canvas,

white,

and the palette behind my eyes is all I need to survive,

all I need to paint you into this absence,

a permanent image of love,

a savior icon in the blinding light of this night's darkness.

CHAPTER TWO
LIFE

OPEN LOVE POEM

(To the memory of the brave and brilliant poet/activist, June Jordan, upon reading her inspiring essay "Besting a worst case scenario" describing her fight with breast cancer).
For Emma (my girasol) for her strength.
Dubai, 10/2008

this poem is a call to arms to trace our
fingers free on the edges of that wound
you wrote about
that wound left unhealed oozing
anger from your
right arm
right armpit
right breast redundant
removed
absent
malignant
that right hand magnificent
which you could no longer move
which was terrifying
like someone had plunged a hole in your chest
    and snatched
out your voice, ripped the veins open and left
you to slowly leak to dying a silent
death,
your words perhaps unwritten unheard

decaying
but you
you with that fighter breath
you found those fingers we all needed
you moved again
you spoke again
you traced that poem
on my open wound that closes with your
thoughts that are
healing
and now you are gone, and i never got the
 chance to say
Thank You
for these words,
for the open friendship
you sought in all of us, after all
this agony, after all these wars you lived
after even all these women you saw
the women bleeding

and i am not black, and i am not dead, and my
breasts are ripe for kissing, for feeding,
for kneading
i am not trying to understand
what bus seat is appropriate for me
but how they could have ever thought your
 voice would be silenced

or forgotten
your scars of mastectomies
and essays and degrees earned by rage, and an assertion that
you are here, and you are the new now, and
all that woman that leaked from all your stitched up
places, a rivulet
unstoppable, an ocean awaits
your courage
your poems a bible for those searching
for common meanings to
the notion of love
how i wish i could have held you, i would have
seen a smile and shaken a hand
and traced a finger over those scars
you were sure would never heal
the veins you thought would never stop seeping

Poet Activist Woman Lover American Mother Teacher
Witch
i bury your words in my interior treasure
i retain forever that hope you died for
i yearn
i mourn

my own mother
whom you would have loved
Palestinian, Teacher, Reader, Sister, Lover, Friend
Witch
and heroine of my wanderlust dreams
in tracing the tubes inserted in her heart, up her nose,
and throat, to let the poison spurt in and out of those now
flat chest surfaces where motherhood remains
and will ever be,
in cleaning those wounds visible
that breath i remember softly quietly fell and rose
and fell again
those sutures not holding together my family
falling apart below
at unspoken seams
and now
ten years later, for your book
i Thank You,
i invoke your words as prayer,
as a blessing for the countless women whose
bodies are reborn into violence
inner
and who edge closer to inward driven fear

and that terminal word
Cancer
how my mother would have loved you,
how i loved cleaning her wounds that are solid
that are real

in your coffin now you are safely a shrouded memory
a sentence of such power and
resistance daring
such simple beauty
in face of a struggle we all need to heed
such blunt honesty
and i Thank You
on this lonely morning
i memorize the words on these pages you left us
despite my wounds inside invisible
despite tears loitering in these eyes
that do not always see
and yet i see
i see you are a brave woman
a vessel of love in unspoken rapture
please,
i want to be your Sister
Daughter
Friend

Student
Poet
Palestinian Comrade
Kindred Warrior
Witch
and i promise you
my wet eyes are still open
and my heart is burdened
but, like yours
it's free
it's free

BEING OF BUTTERFLIES

For Toots, who is a grand character.
Beirut, 12/2007

Milan suggested that poems
are found
behind the thin veneer
of our faces searching
for a valid reason to exist

and poets capture them, little desires
behind our thoughts
as would
an avid collector
reigning in poems floating unbounded
by our flesh
our steady stride towards death
our ideas mostly mortal
trapped in language
and ailing hands
as we wither

and yet poetry is there
behind our eyes so bland
firmly grasping onto lives
we may find tenuous

as an addict would
i am here
to pay homage
to Milan and his countless peers
who also suffer
the novelists baring depths of
our incompetence
in works so grand
they stand as pillars of eternal
remembrance of a sacred hand
and they leave butterflied flowers
wreathing my hair
strand after intoxicated
strand

i, addicted,
armed with a net
of ink so fine
dry
as a vulture i roam paths
behind my eyes
to devoutly conjure you
to pin down a winged poem of you
perhaps
my brown eyed lover
to fasten you in pages

LIFE

in lines that flit and flutter
pages to revere those ink explorers who
my respect and fascination command
and demand

those drowning voyagers of
inner water and sky and sand

i, the nonbeliever
kneel for
those who came before
and left
and left their words
in time immortal
in a memorial to all that they have attained
in majesty to stand
and be able to
loudly
say

UNTITLED

For Maamoun.
Beirut, undated

What does it matter
to fill up endless sheets of white
paper screens
that are flawless, the tip of a pen an
experience in clenched control
and rapture
but what does it matter
i am committed to repeating
endless follies of curves
and lines in words
i mutter and utter and stutter
sobbing
it does not matter
all the words i decried
this silence we watch the earth unravel
it does not matter
i could rot with my wrist burnt upon
this page
ink still flows in syntax
and grammatical thunder, error after
vacant error,
in my veins nothing but a memory

of terror
and what does it matter

somewhere in palestine
iraq
sudan or ethiopia
yemen or south america
in the heart of beirut
where i stammer and blunder
growing fatter
on useless jargon junk and trashy
banter
chatter

somewhere in this world
a child is hungry
and she hurts,
she hurts.

BECOMING POETRY

For Tai, who gives me beautiful spaces.
New York, 09/2008

until i am inspired by merely the breath alive
in no imposed conscious desire
until i can clearly paint the orbit of the stars
around your smile
those veins we all share
despite enemies and
differences assumed
and wars declared
until i can hear the din of your thoughts
    landing
safely on mine, i cannot venture forth
an understanding total of
the meaning of
the verb to write

bad opening stanzas converge to plot in
me this desire to try
for until i can muscle up the heart to follow
    each
thought speeding to the center of that abyss
we name memory
how filled with sorrow it is this

LIFE

graveyard of images habitual, hard it
is to rescue these
thoughts
we deem precious we deem vital
we deem immortal after the seconds they stay
death comes quick to words that are fragile
they that deserve the paper shroud are few
    and
far from the empty fullness of the mind

and until i learn to save a child from the lives
    spent in fear
until i can hollow out that throbbing section
of hurt on your face
until i can scavenge and retrieve every painful
    trace
of life's blows to your space
embrace away the frown you wear at dusk
every toss unpleasant of our shared sleep
until you no longer weep without knowing
    why
until i eradicate those cries, of every
single forgotten child, until the calm can
stain and continue to seep
peace
until love is the only possible answer to the
questions our hearts grasp and keep

unless i summon all that in the flick of a spell-weaving
wrist, then open wide my fingers to hold your hand
till all the healing words run steady
stay deep
this cannot be named the journey to write

deceased poems taunt me on a bewitched night
they float around unfocused
ripe for the picking but
well out of this sour woman's way
they taint the stillness of an urban night, another
morn to wake up empty
until i can burst open, kinetically
magnetically
aligned with all the hopes you muster at the start of each work
week, harried
and forlorn and abandoned are we to desks and uniforms and
forgotten language of the old raw methods as
we inspire and expire in a new universe
silent
i tire of holding this net for poems to catch

LIFE

my hair a nest of fire
eyes stuck in the mire of banality
and fingers tapping to rule a miniscule empire
i tire, and drive forth the will
to abandon this hunt
admit to the feeble kill
and only then, when i immerse my lungs
in words and paper to render
me blind, until the yoke of this ink has strangled me
i am shackled long and deep and wide
and cannot hide the predator inside
until i am a full captive of myself
alone coercing poems out of flight
until then
until i can guard the love we all
need to hide, and abide by the laws of metaphysics
betrothed to kindness, and the madness of lives spent wiping
words off all the dirty surface
until then, until the reconciliation between neurons
arching impulses that are poison
all these letters in time spent alone
until i am free to be
the owner of myself, all facets pressed and

dried and collected
like a flower picked by a sad bride
on her wedding night, to be that flower that shelters you
for years brushed aside by
death
and until i am declared a woman losing her mind
by those who have seen it before
until i can roar in the whispers i send to you
that i want to write
i must first be taught to court the stars at night
to twist the moon
into shapes that while away the unslept time
till finality explains itself to me
in laymen terms i can respect and admire
until then
until i figure out
why cells wont obey me, until i can verbally
emphatically put down in letters you may translate
everything we need to know about love
and hate
until then i can only say i tried, and i tried and tried

until the spiritual stories make sense to me

LIFE

and are real, not role-playing characters that are so far

imaginary, because one must believe in something

ultimately, and until i can trust to believe what

my eyes don't see

until we can quantify love, and describe what

it is to just be, until we measure the weight

of friendship on scales of our entwined palms

until we convince the resurrection daily of another day

to stop being the only way

i must find my own means to pray, to yearn for the flesh to say

and ask for and receive another brand new

day, only then, when i am filled with queries no longer

and clear is the home in which i am to stay

then you can proclaim

hey

she would have done well to try and write

until you love me beyond the decay day by day

of my hair and skin organs voice smell laugh kiss fuck hold

and eyes

and say,

always that melodious death of our say
vocal chords extinguished in a harmony of silence
that is the only way, only then when we can
sing all that we need to pray
i will write to you then
to tell you i love you too

no matter the decay

only when the earth explains herself in languages familiar
in long winded dreams of our nights, sobriety
astray
in short bursts of song that is the music
enabling life
enabling my desire to stay
when all the sound clusters to dwell in soundtracks
of beauty, when i am starry and
alight, when this is my gift
to myself, drifting to spaces leaving the soil
to trek the mysterious pages that are vile
adversaries of anyone wanting to write and write and drift aloft
the letters that only you can say
until that day
writing falls always short of my voices that

stray
and only when and only if, only how, i can come to know
how quick your feelings come in and go, to know
how i can traverse the distance between hopes
and words, in all the unworded chatter
our skin buzzes, when that geography
of minutiae tells me about the crests and valleys
in your chest, breathing in love for me
when the seas are but a fraction of our home together, only then,
lover, friend or family
stranger in nights smiling, strangers but for the pen,
only then can one dare to try and write

until i can stop time from winning
always spinning stories to steal my seconds
to find the immortality
one needs to willfully awake in mornings
futility lingering a cobweb of fear to trap me here
arms bound, eyes extinguished
death a mere breath away

until until until i can still
the cries of every child buried in the lives
    spent in fear,
until i can hollow out that throbbing section
of hurt on your face
until then,
i cannot ever really write

and so
and so what
and what if
what does all this wanton seeking say
about what you and i are doing
right now, here in this precious time we have
    not killed
memories of words to ever stay
even if only for

today

know this
know that this is all i am left to say
know that i love you
today
and know how
my love comes to me invisible
loud and clear to convey

everything we try to place on the insides
of our space, in every trace outline of thought
 you left behind
lied in divinity, beside
everything else sacred inside
outside
your gorgeous mind
is reborn to life, forever and ever more
and is
becoming poetry

everything we try not to say, that we leave
 behind, to die
on the edges of our infinite way, all of that
which my fingers cannot bring
to you
all that ever bathed in light and dark
to span the horizon which is etched for
 evermore
is for now, and forever
at your core
even your savage inhuman core
is alive
is your own indelible mark
and is
becoming poetry

FOR THE RECORD

For my students who cared about their world.
Beirut, 06/2008

I could not tell if her panties were red
the video-clip was amateur, reality as some choose to make it
fuzzy, replayed on screens
our hearts betrayed
the red seeped from wounds in forbidden places, i
could not breathe, she crawled to hide
in muffled cries, nowhere to go
that open space of fury she inhabits

We sat in silence and watched her head get
cracked in by a brotherhood of kin
and by unsanctioned love, and by family that lunged
stones instead of hugs
creating shrouds of honor and revenge in death
i forced air softly,
in and out, counting
to not vomit
please,
i cannot vomit

LIFE

Try to stem those hateful tears i gathered
we witnessed
the descending darkness that circled these
cries of savages who barked out
Animal Animal
they named her
huddled in a ball protected by her arms that have once held
a man who loved her, a virgin still, perhaps
a young carcass bludgeoned pulpy
by family in throes of religious idiocy
maybe she and her man were not from the same sect
or political party
or country
maybe she accepted the universe wide in her young heart and
found the cage in her Arabian desert
had locked her tight, it was too late
bars around her aplenty
fervent insanity and years of patriarchy, the absence of a kind
merciful God
in their eyes of fire holy
incanting my damnation
and madness, and insecurity, their demons forcing acts

of lunacy and yet they dare call her, and
her young sacred love
heresy

And now
all is once again proper
family honor intact
restored from the bleeding thighs of this young daughter
i wonder if her name was Mariam or Fatima or Leila or Hannah
what is her smile like, beyond the view
of her matted hair, that heavy head lolling
oblivious, arms squeezed
curled up burning on the coals of history
Animal Animal is what she becomes
her last beat of a heart meets with expiry
without ever having understood
how a family can do this
how love can lead to such suffering
where did it come from
all this apathy

As you drove bricks into her cracked frame
again and again you yelled the same old name
hiding your misery inner, that fear you can
never proclaim

Animal Animal

while my tears ran
trying to stomach this violence
trying to remain intact
to figure out
how your allahu akbar plays into this scene,
    how can it
how can you dare repeat it coupled in savagery
with your hearts, in your loins, around these
    arms of carnage
through your faces smothered with illiteracy
Thud Thud Thud
went the stone brick, into her
temples, cheeks, nose splintered, eyes sunk in
into her future, and her womb, empty and
robbed in an everyday
modern tragedy, and like some dark, surreal
comedy someone thought to cover her bare
ass, pulled up her skirt,
colored with spit and heartache and dirt
dragged through sand and sea to
salt this unhealed wound in my heart
and this is no animal kingdom documentary
no late night show of the wild
this is Iraq,
Jordan
Egypt

112   Africa Asia Europe and the States
these are my sisters, dead on soil and sand and kitchen floors,
abused
laid as waste
these are the stories of women
wide eyed and aching
restless, living in tension
nervously

This what happens when a man decides whom we can love
and how and when,
why i can share my body and under what rules,
bought or sold by a relative who is male,
bought and sold according to commandments written by
ancient men in popular books of mythology
bought and sold by 21st century fools
who think they know the tools
to handle me
who think they draw the confines of my captivity
and this is what happens when
a man believes he is excused
allowed, encouraged, or even just lightly

    rebuked, slapped
on the wrist for wanting further proof
of how honor has been reinstated now that
this whore and her stain of betrayal has been removed,
this is what happens when a man can
videotape my murder on his brand new phone cam
to later on brag and prove
we fucking got that bitch man,
we gave it to her right,
she deserved it, too
i got it all here on tape man, you can see her ass
a little, and there is tons of blood,
we got her good man,
it took fourteen of us, three bricks,
and some heavy boots,
we got her, we didn't even have to use the sticks.
Fucking whore, little cunt thought she would split
with him, we got her, little shithead
aint moving
another
fucking
inch.

The red snakes of her sins
slither out across those dunes of hate
her blood is absorbed
to smudge this barren Arab soil around us
a smear of shame
i shiver
her spirit transcends into our tearful state
it invades the flinching pain in me
gut acrid in hate
it shoots up revolt in the clenched jaw of my anger,
it fumes up the air stagnant with cataclysmic power,
and i,
i want a weapon to bury you with motherfuckers
i want a saw to cut off
these arms you wield, you dumbfucks, my hands a blaze of fire
to char your frigid face
i want a hammer to hack out your entrails
i want a gun to blow holes where your balls might have been
i want to choke your misguided pulse, leave nothing

of life in you, not
even a trace
i want to chop that smug head of yours right
    off, and still even then
deep in your gut i want to smear
endless pain
and i want to say and say and endlessly
    exclaim
look at me, you murderer
check me out, you fucker
here i am, here I AM
and don't you forget these words, ever

her life is not yours for the taking
her life is not yours for the taking

Even your God says this to you in your gospels
    of hate
her dreams are not yours to command and
    rape and erase
listen to me
look at me
and i'll tell you this
from the dregs of history
from my own inner sanctuary
stronger than your sadist army
from the hard heart i carry within me

life will not go on this way
life cannot go on this way.

Soon enough, you will see, without the
sacred feminine powers at play
this world is in imbalance
and without acceptance and
tranquility
we will annihilate humanity
and in the ashes of a nuked world we once
   loved
tell me not brother of your holy wars
tell me not of honor in families adored and
   restored
tell me not of your male responsibility
her life is not yours for the taking
and you will not tell me
who to love and when and how
for love itself is a deity
and love triumphs no matter how many
   women you cleanse
no matter how many smiles you snuff
no matter how long it takes for you to
remember
that enough is enough and these women
who could be

LIFE

your mother and sister and cousin and lover,
are all earth and her heavens,
are all the stars and their luster
they are the safety net that holds up the sky,
they are that soft whisper murmuring inside
 you, lost.

They are the daughters of life,
and at the same time
life's ancestry.

How could you then, in the light of day, that
 light that
God gave you to shine your masculine way,
how could you stray
how could you stay so deeply astray
how could you fear
how could you despise us so much?

The video clip ends.

I can breathe
and in me,
inside me, love
is tired and damaged
yet
picks itself off the kitchen floor, and through

the soil
through the sand
of the promise of a new day
love
unfurls again in hope
a lotus blossoms
i pray
i pray
i pray.

MANIFESTO

Beirut, 04/2008

Someone must stop them
those who bang war drums round our homes
this cannot be the only way
someone must stop them
i am a coward
i will not die for your absence
your silence
but someone must stop them
we do not have much time
our world is sitting on a ledge
legs ready to jump
we watch from the dirty bathroom
razor blades wait at the
defeated edges of our wrists
asking if we are
ready

PATIENCE

Beirut, 11/2007

today
Abed
the young man who cleans my building
whose cigarette trails wisp out of his one-room
yellow home in the lobby
his TV loud, unwatched
the bare walls he once asked me to help fill
in some artsy manner
after i said welcome
you're new here
hope you are ok
hope you will be able to stay

Abed
the man who nervously asked for the electric bill
and gave me a weary look when i asked for
the plumber for the fifth time
the man who held the magical key
to the power switch castle
where sudden Beirut dark electrical failure
can be cast away

LIFE

the man who made me trudge back and forth
swearing tight-lipped
fuming
to find him feasting with his bro in the adjacent
apartment building
Ramadan casting its new rules over
those of my comfort
Abed
who always managed to help in the end

today
Abed
stood outside his door beaming
giving me the most jovial of all greetings
and as i smiled back
handing over the usual payment for this and that
i noticed
aside from the gleam in his eye

Abed was wearing glitter

not enough for cross dress purposes
or other such revelry
but a tiny hint of glimmer
traced his lit up eyes

and he said
guess what
i got married

i brought her and came

and i said,
what?
when were you gone?
three days you say?
maybe i too was away

she's here now, come look
her name is Nisrine

and she was indeed there
smiling shuffling slowly out of the door to meet me
little sparkles in her pretty eyes
long scarves hiding her face
her curves
any scars

and as i welcomed her
gently teasing, offering them my sincerest
warm feelings

i could not help reeling

i could not help stealing a glimpse of what it was like
to be under someone
legs wide
heart ragged
hair unbound and fingers your flesh kneading
a stranger breathing half words of lunacy
to your virgin
hearing
and how it is to not know the patience of slow love

today
Abed was grinning deeply
at his three day wedding expedition
tomorrow he will hold his precious daughters in smoky fingers
and sweaty arms of instinctive love
and Nisrine will hopefully still smile
at me
and help him with the everlasting cleaning cleaning cleaning

and i could not help
envy with all the envy my dark heart could

take
how do i know it's a mistake
a three-day marriage contract
children burst forth from tradition
and all its jurisdiction

and how
how do they accept so easy
arms around you, breathless
feeding children together
speaking
chores daily
and the same routine every evening
and how
how do they maintain smiles
make it so easy
how can it be so easy

and why oh why
when so many years are spent
exploring
adoring
abhorring
why oh why

do you and i make it so difficult.

MAPS

Beirut, 10/2007

Words have connected brush stroke fingers
to my cheek
in letters oblivious to their constructions
and power
we have found our common habitat of
lines
swirls
curvy shaped dotted felt-tipped needs that
    flow
and leak
Words that leave a bruising burning ink jet
    streak
Words defiant
impish
Words errant and stranded
Words frantic
tender
Words that are traces of all that was
and lives no longer
Words to render me silent
render me without knowledge of my name
my age
my face

my gender
Words so tender
Words creating a day to be
a death to foresee
Words sketching you to me
to ask and fret and beg to see
to comprehend the end of me inside of me
and Words, despite being so smart and careless
and free
Words that do not ever reveal themselves
to explain death
no matter to what universe I plea
Words that allow the world to see
first worlds allowed to be
Words in me locked up
Words in me exploding in emotions that flee
Words Words to hypnotize me
to tranquilize me.

Words to seek shelter for eyes
grown accustomed
growing wise
and weary of all the untold lies
Words personal in size
Words private hovering around my thighs

LIFE

Words replacing mental cries
Words to jail
uninhibited
skies.

Words to care
Words to tumble out in dirges
in our sweat and silky urges
in our oft unfocused morbid stare
Words to say what the fingers cannot
say what my ankles adorned
cannot say when bare
Words to retrace moments of splendor rare
Words to tear and tear
to ensnare
all your fleeting whims freed in a courageous
    dare
Words to share
the mundane
to groan ecstasy hands grasped tugging in the
    motion of my hair.
Words to care.

Words to violently cry
Words rapid even when my throat is aflame
is dry
Words so fucking elusive when high

Words so effusive
Words on the fly
Words when the veins nurturing dreams
seeping have run dry
Words to peek and pry
Word to reek and seek and try and try
Words to whisper a hello my love
Words to slam shut a good bye.

Words fluttering in color away
flying out of eyes astray
Words to stumble out unhampered
searching for safe lands in your hands
playgrounds where it's allowed to play
a lonely beach where they can sun
they can rest a little
they can stay
Words that stray
in our dawn drenched Milky Way
Words that peek out of fingers
in movement of tiny creatures nestled in nature's hay
and Words to send me enchanted songs
Words to weep out absences
Words that pray
that long

that whither and mourn the length
of our doomed path
our dead-end mortal way
Words to clasp your waist abundant and
Words to push fear away
Words hiding in all the mornings of love
when our smiles knew not what to further say.

Words that you hear
such words that you intimately
so singularly fear
Words that tinge and singe and sear
and Words exchanged trivial
Words as disposable as peanut shells we toss
    out
out in nights for a midnight beer
all the Words that leer
in dusks unmasked I am in your arms
your eyes my horizon
breath carefully poised in my heart
and your heat near.

Words that only you hear
Words held close for day
safeguarded softly for a year
buried in treasure trunks year after year after
    year

far past the letters on lover paper
dead love a mere old stained smear
and Words that you hold dear
the magic words, ancient,
that are all that
you can still hear.

Finally,
Words useless to stretch out
minutes without you
lonely
Words to eternally commit and proclaim
that I love you
Words flung out in battles to exclaim
that I love you
in Words divine
in Words holy
Words parting hell
for spirits chanting all our story
in all the Words
we ever needed to tell

Words to keep you with me
simple and plain

oh for Words to not even have to explain.

VOCATION: REVOLUTION

For Ethelbert Miller.
Dubai, 15/11/2009

They will tell you
you are a poet because you have flaming red hair
and sleep till noon just because you
like dreaming
and rolling over alone in a bed, musky,
refuting the world intruding when it damn pleases
they will tell you
you are a poet because the words are
little tidal waves that swallow screens of desolation,
filling to the brim all the eye can bear to see
all the mind can bear to remember,
they will tell you that you are a poet because you
smoke too many cigarettes,
or drugs, or drink hard straight liquor like a cowboy,
when you are a Middle Eastern female, and required
to be more modest
or because your suitcases are always

open, a sock never matching the
other one you scramble to find,
or because you are late,
time plays its own magic tricks on you, and entire months
have gone by with no weight
they will tell you
you have the language
you can rhyme
you are great because like modern
spoken word prophets
you refuse to rhyme
they will tell you
it's your wicked sense of observation
it's the details in your hands caressing all you can touch,
it's your lack of public awareness,
your creation of a story from a handshake, the glimmer in your
eyes when laughter rocks your sinews
they will tell you
You are a Poet
because you wear large robes with color
and beads
and you don't even know what's on the label,
you must then be a poet
they say

LIFE

people read you
they blush
they cry
you publish
you print
you try
you think in hyperbole
you orgasm in metaphors of lands holy
you regard your toes for hours wondering at that miracle
you bow down before the perfection of children
you must, then, be a poet
you have ink stains where others have polish
you have bitten lips where others kiss gloss
you have a body not fit not lean not hard
a soft body
as soft as keystrokes
as wide as language
as pliable as the imagination
they will tell you all the reasons why you are a poet,
and they may be right each time,
but only you will know,
only the poet knows that poetry
is not words
strung

it is the act of illuminating the best in every
    reading tongue,
it is the gift to let others decipher what is the
    inner name
they call themselves
it is the silence after the last line is devoured
and the here now creeps back in
but i say
we are only poets when we scream in letters
bearing witness for all the
hurt subdued voices
otherwise to remain
unsung

ALL SAINTS

For Scott, who is never in costume, with gratitude.
Dubai, 31/10/2008

the ones with curly hair, not curly like mine
but frizzy, with that skin i covet
black, maybe brown
they with the rhythm in their soles
sit wound up tightly
in groups
i glance around me
dubai midnight blues
the blond and blue-eyed hunt for flesh
no longer wary
booze our armor of the evening
civil acts forcing them to keep mixed
but marginalized yet
company
carrying beers they forgot they bought, louder than
they need to be heard
unruly, in groups also, their women giggle
and teeter on the edges
of undeserved paychecks
of high heeled sexiness
and discomfort inner

oblivion
and in groups, the ones with eyes slanted simmer
they quiet, they dimmer
they observe us, a pantomime orgiastic
pleasure pursued trivial
and i shiver
and it's hot
and it's humid
and crowded and beer after beer
is bitter
and i am no closer to understanding
why all these colors don't blend in
together
like some sexy tie-dye sweater
they don't wash and tumble and roll into one another
like how it should be
maybe even
better
and i wonder
do vampires bully
the pakistani or the arab they
think is nasty? What about zombies, are they choosy about what color flesh they
devour
and what of ghouls, and what of ghosts?

i surrender
to the class divisions
like incisions
in my skin
sometimes white
sometimes brown
sometimes golden
and shiny
to seek the collision of life
that does not happen here, that space between
what our DNA
cannot say
that stamp of appearances that
they deem holy
truly
truly,

there is a ghoul inside us
and a costume outside
fake,
cheap, and silly.

FRIEND

For Amer, who carries our history, with so so much love.
Dubai, 01/02/2009

You knew me before I was this woman
poet scrounging for words
elusive
witnessing together the triumph
of that journey we took to
become us, in the making, ever and
again, unmade and replaced by
a newer carcass
lost to our youth, how your smile still dazzles
me and sends me letters in silence
across distance we
never paid attention to,
you knew me awkward and afraid
attuned to the tacit agreements we
signed to love beyond the
geography of convenience
beyond the shape of the atlas
beneath the earth that separates, to dwell in the
quickened internal rhapsody
of your fleeting poems, a prayer, an amulet to protect our laughter

LIFE

burying the days of despair we count over and
  over
brutal score keepers noting each other's
  failure
my fingers unclenched to protect you
from yourself
I am bare,
that hideous form I cower from dispelled in
  the mirror
of your hands, for
to you, I am no shape
I am no matter
but a collection of stars free in your night
a simple sun ray beaming through a window of
  time
stretching to where you stand solid
that lights the horizon of memory
from here
to there, to you. And now I am tempted to cup
  my hand
across your face, to lean in and touch
the absence of distance, to mold
my thoughts after the
pattern of our speech, frazzled,
connected through stutter and the singular
  way
there is no other like you,

none ever. You keep my past safe in renewed breath,
I forage the world to dream close to you
willing this life to break
gently
a tumbleweed of love fragile
to be swept up
in the free wind
together

MANTRA

New York, 06/2004

Dawn sneaks into my home
and it marches in
this murder we call sunlight
each ray bringing death closer as I understand time.
As I come to hate time.

Time
wrinkles
scars
deep set burn marks to end my youth
no matter what is said
or what vitriol you scream,
ugly creation lives on
each summer morning buries a dream.

Skin goes first you know.
Our largest organ once held us so tightly,
now
now it lets go slowly till one dark day
no one hesitates or even stops mid stride
to marvel
nor pray to the youth shining out of your eyes.

You become tired
the sun etches lines you could not erase
even if you tried.

Oh you who know the secrets of life
tell me why
the flesh caves,
but the spirit won't?
A lost battle from birth, your breath and
the damn sun march on
ever in motion
towards a place infinitely far yet so near
the space of death
unreal.

And when my eyes, once speaking
in brown tongues of furor
when they spark out soundless in a second
what is it
that they see?

Tell me why
you who know the spirits
tell me why the sun moves on
why the moon talks to us every night
tell me why life holds on, despite me, my

LIFE

    sagging flesh
my every day fight

And tell me,
tell me how to have children
how to hand them my plight.

It makes us love,
this unstoppable machine that is life.

It sends the soul the loins the lips and ears
out to howl your name.
Oh chance
bring my man home to me
bring him tonight.
Bring him to kiss me
to touch the body that is growing to die.
Bring him tonight.

The sun smirks, comes up to full bloom.

Oh you who know of love, tell me
tell me how to stop the sun
how to kill the moon.

Tell me where my man is,

144 let all the ageless stars bring him home.

Oh you who know of death
tell me why
like everything else
does love have to die.

LIFE

SCHOOL TRIP NIGHTS

For Denise and Nuria, warm, laughing and whole.
(and Emile).
Dubai, 14/2/2010

This is the slow burn of loving beyond sanity

up at 12 eighteen in dark Dubai making

cupcakes for a daughter who couldn't

get that recipe right

enough

to not embarrass her in front of friends at school who

eat chocolate as if it were just there

as if tired hands didn't bake till the eyes

went hot and

puffy.

This is the slow burning of love you carry to a grave

the desire to show your child what

mother is, what child is, what

this equation can rise in your center like

hot sweet yeast

even misshapen

even crumbling off the edges, a toil of last minute rescue

for her wide eyes in need

this is the slow burning of love beyond reason,

after dinner, in silence
we smell the vanilla of her young smile in the morning
teeth brown and comfort.

This is a mother,
this is loving beyond nature,
we bake and a child learns of the inside of a heart
a child learns of all that is sacred.

PUBLIC READINGS

For Suheir Hammad, gorgeous.
Dubai, 12/2/2010

This is how poets are born.
Sit in back rooms of secluded structures while
 a single mic blasts
your sorrow from where you buried it
dredges everything you hid to fill this damp
room with minerals precious
that feeling
of coming home to a place you never knew
you never knew you could love this hard
listen to open veins reading the personal
a light wraps bodies tethered free
shed the person you wore in the sunlight
 outside
or a nighttime laugh you sent out to the city
 before
this room becomes all of Manhattan
and her windows.
This is how love is spun,
glance into the eyes of someone you could
 touch beyond hands and skin
repeat words wordless burrowed you could
 flood out
a kiss has you grappling for a dictionary of

terms uncoined
and one day, a poem, a poem comes to you, says all you can ascribe
to one moment, one person, fills a universe complete

you know, this is what I wanted to say
this is what I have always wanted to say.

The person you love understands
or not
but no matter
firmly in its place poetry has rooted explanation
this is real
this is the life blooms
fits
is seized
deciphered and true.

This is how a poet is born.

CHAPTER THREE
HOME

CIVIL FATIGUES

For my friends who love Falasteen despite any and everything.
Beirut, 03/2008

i am so tired of you palestine

they told us you were ours
yet i saw the light for the first time
in lands akin to yours
close but not yours
they told me when i could open my eyes
that you were full of wonder
men women lived as angels under your trees
they told me fairy tales of princes that kneeled
mad with love
on their knees
they told me you were bountiful
generous
glamorous
an atheist
some said sacredly religious
some say dark
and magical
they said you carved the stories
of all the myths possible

to shelter humanity
your perfection
complete
flawless
you were the essence of their trinity
the word that came before we knew of this silence
the water of river adorning you
holy water absorbed in your femininity
they told me lie after lie of your proximity to god
to all that is love
to all that is divinity

i am so tired of you palestine
the lies i was told in line
after poetic line
the gossip you promoted with such impunity
about green lands of delicious fantasy
where soil exploded not in craters of fire
but into food for hungry bellies
miracles daily
rumors of your continuous gaiety
your exquisite brown-eyed children
limbs embracing the sun
flinging hearts in abandon
throwing not rocks

HOME

but glances of joy
free
careless
not one blue and white striped wolf in the
 vicinity

oh palestine, how they crafted you
spun stories to douse your
demise with pantomimes
acted out for our entertainment, our popcorn
fiesta oblivious while they
hid your unlawful
ungodly captivity
the bloodshed
shed hourly
on your scene of nativity
i am so tired of you palestine,
i am so tired of your master capturers
and their den of global iniquity

for every growing luminous tree
witnessed in my imagined dreams of you
you offered a corpse at dawn

for every child free
i could have blossomed forth

HOME

you offered me curses
hate-filled chants of infertility

where arms should have held in brown amber
strength in male beauty
in compassion
humility
where i saw courage in men
i loved from villages burnt
from refugee camps filled plenty
from camps ravaged
second time empty
i yearned for kindred tender masculinity
a traveler of your journey
palestine
and you offered betrayal
at best
at the most you offered
heartless frigidity

and i am so tired of learning you falasteen,
i am tired of spelling your name differently
of pronouncing Arabic in accents all jumbled
of not speaking your language properly
of trying to locate your borders

HOME

my own checkpoints caged
my roads home a maze
i am done chasing useless positivity
there is none of you left for me
to blend in with my genetic chemistry
you denied me a birth
a nationality
you will not sow my death as your own
as proof of your star spangled virility

no, no ya falasteen...how
how they have made even your name
a profanity

i am so tired falasteen,
tired of knowing you superficially
never unearthing your mystery
in our affair of clenched hearts
and insanity
your mountains, illusions of smoke
your breezes, a fog of rancid heavy density
they have warped you my love
they have you reborn
an atrocity
a genetic mutation
of defective

machinery of monstrosity

i am tired of your mood swings
hammering on my heart strings
tired of inner conflicts crushing your people
dumb appeals to a barren
united nations of inanity

no one loves you anymore falasteen
your streets a collection of fables
with morals about their depravity
your homes a battle ground
for savages to assert their
flawed identity
for savages to rip apart
our selfishness
our weaknesses
our cowardice, you fucking Arabs
our lack of tenacity

no one loves you,
no one ya falasteen
maybe not even me

i am tired of you
palestine,

HOME

i cannot even commit you to a dumpsite
of memory
a past buried in private graveyards
i cannot string words to
honor you
with at least a eulogy
i cannot say how we feel about you,
you
a child
a parent
rival, friend, enemy
a load, a burden
a neighbor, a lover
a fruit tree you are palestine
decaying at the root of every heart-broken
split apart family

i am so tired of living with you
of your life inside me
invisibly
the articles of your wardrobe
replete with beads of suffering
every morning you dress me with terror
you feed me lunacy
and massacres
and tragedy

HOME

every evening you shed dead skin
you glow with soft caresses of lingering
    stubborn memory
i looked for a home
you bequeathed me vagabond stories
and where i thought to grow roots
to plant camaraderie
you flooded with steel, and six edged stars
of madness
of evil empires and their immortality

your marriage of tradition
ignorance
and greed has left us slumped in a bed
stains on our thighs
looking for remnants of our
gang banged
loss of
virginity

oh palestine, you tire me
you offer the senses nothing to cling to
    anymore
in this sea of frailty…
you no longer exist on this map of injustice
the murder details of your million years
etched into a history

of life and ancestry
is now salon talk of
poor woman
isn't it so terrible
all these dead children
what to do what to do
smoke smoke drink drink breath choked
eyes extinguished in inferiority

the mass genocide of you falasteen
no longer news worthy of being obscene
has become silent hate festering
has become daily banality

at what point does one lose track of the dead?
do we stop counting?

oh palestine, your numbers tire me
our land gets smaller,
the graphs of settlers settling old scores
rising so healthy
such assurance indicated in figures
such growth rate
our fragility
their solidity
while you starve ya falasteen,

while you stumble begging
blind
limping
bordering on the edge of suicide
and its welcome finality

how do we laugh at life's cruelty?
what kind of joke are they, these Israelis?

i am so tired of your math palestine,
your losses and gain
full of pain
and added pain
till all i am is numb
all i witness but absurdity

i am so tired ya falasteen,
i am tired of loving you
and hating you
and loving you
fundamentally
intrinsically
instinctively
eternally

IN BED WITH AMERICA
New York, 10/2008

i find the green is faded on the other side
of your lips
i have but a few well rehearsed lines to say
the blonde and blue march by me blind
the laughter is loud
and vacant
music always distorted
cheeks that ache in the effort of inbuilt smiles
i am away from the arms that are simple,
and the brown eyes, quiet, and yet
often
wild
rampant with touch that i favour,
a flavour of thyme
and your lips that are full, that are ripe and my
thoughtless fingers on your waist
a twisted addicted
vine

america is but a frame of an illusion
i have still
in the solitary space
i can glide through time

but it is not for me this
privileged ennui
the curtain is always pushed aside for a show
i find monotonous
what is there to smile at when there
is no need to cry
and i dont cry
the men are still lost, stretched out silent beneath
my rented matchbox
a fine paid for the freedom i perceive
is rightfully mine in
america
i am not free to heal them
i am at the checkout aisle wanting more items at a dollar ninety nine
i am but a whisper of myself in these cackling streets
beauty is a vengeance here
it lashes out with pent up
speed
it is too much to drown me in
options and choices and variety
without clarity
transient desire tires me
i am a credit card melting into my skin
disappearing in the lull of the ebb of natural

humanity

maybe it is all just as it once was
maybe it is just i who is heavy
sinking into the once greener land
loaded with the universal weight
of love being open wide
inside

COURAGE, INCH BY INCH

For Chris Michael, who loves Beirut.
Beirut, 02/2008

beirut
you leave me no room to
fret and pace
and ponder
in creative spaces
reflective
garnering joy to my inner thrive
the personal sacred
perspective
you squeeze me against polluted
razor-edged places
tight
getting darker

i am beaming light
i am pure laughter

beirut
the pastures in my hands
fear you not
it does not matter
how many a wasted martyr

HOME

you sacrifice
to your gods of feudal trash
and stench and garbage-tainted matter
how many noise filled
seconds of harshness
you impose
how many burn marks you ignite
you plunge in knives of invasive insipid
banter
go
go tell the grating construction of your frail
denizens that bang and screw and drive and
    hammer
as they flounder and falter
say
all your echoing daily thrusts of anger
threaten not to overcome
cannot ever drown down
pitches of private
rapture

beirut
you do not scare me
try,
try your damndest
weep, moan, shake and cry

fill my early
bleary
mornings love lost weary
bequeath me all your broken silence
all the cruelty you can muster
i am root and tree and leaves swaying
i do not fluster

beirut
you have shed your dignity
your clothes
revealing scarred and decaying
nudity
you caged in lovers
in cramped untidy
traces
of lives held back by
death and theft and greed
and anguished bravery
this the flour in your bread
this the demon lover in your bed
the songs of your street
move your people
in trances
unreal unalive undead

HOME

beirut
you do not own me
you cannot steer me
i am the field of life unveiling
in harmony blooming
and you,
you are a maze of cluster bombs
beauty ravaged,
now only appearing
in seconds fleeting
not enough
not enough
to keep me breathing
to enable sight taste touch hearing
dreaming

beirut
you have sent me jilted
i am left free
bearing peace within me
flaunting love embossed on me,
and you beirut,
you of the now barren soil
charred
subdued
murdered daily

170   you
       you do not feel me.

PICK ME UP

For Palestine, who defies geography.
Dubai, 11/2008

Smiles freeze, drop off the faces of strangers who
try their pick up lines of sleaze on
trains through France, who see
a redhead
made up in tight
clothes that show off the curves
international, woman, all throughout, and they
inevitably ask, where
are you from, and watching the eyes widen,
in dismay sometimes, sometimes in respect
often in pity, always a controversy
always an opinion, I'm with you, I'm with them, you don't exist,
they should never have existed, but you're
so pretty, said with surprise, like
i am supposed to be ugly,
how strange, your accent is all perfect and you
don't look funny, and by funny,
they mean swathed in black
mourning and veils
wailing murder and disease and misery

and if i smile in secret knowledge of the diversity of my
ancestry, do not hold it
against me, for there
is little left of that today
this day of humiliation
this black morning that wont cease, those clouds of doom
that wont blow
and when someone asks where your aunt is,
when some official wants to know
who's this uncle, and how come you live alone
aren't you an Arab young woman, why are you
traveling so far from home, and where were
you born, and what passport do you hold, and how come your accent
is all fucked up,
because Mr. official man with too much time on your hands
i have languages for every occasion
different words
in different situations to the rescue, i play
the right card
at every given chance to
make sure one gets by, one gets the best, in this racist
test of endurance, you say,

you're from here, but born there, and you don't know
where your uncle is, and you haven't met
all your thirty three cousins
and there is a grandparent who never saw you
and you speak not the same language as your sister in law
nor do you run into the same family name, and when the villages
of your friends are their retreat for this Christmas
or Eid, or this or that festivity
you keep your head down, you look up plans on expedia
for an itinerary as random as
you wish it to be, for your village might have been
bulldozed flat by those powers that be,
that you know inside out,
cannot be, should not be
and yet they are, here, and were, and will to stay,
they think, eternally.

And you grieve,
daily
and you did not hold your father's hand when your mother

died, and you did not go to the funeral of the only
grandmother you ever knew or loved
and you may not make it to the wedding of your
favorite cousin, and you cannot tell if they will grant you
the visa for that scholarship
you deserve and need and you don't know
if you can remember all the names of family,
distant, and you cannot remember how your father took the news
of his own parents dying
years after the fact, because no one knew
where he was or how to tell him
the news
over the telephone your life is lived
and emails become your heirlooms of jewels
and pictures are what you make do
with night after morning
of absence

and you wish

you wish you held your father's heart
when your mother died
but he was not there

HOME

and you could not remove that hurt stare
he has on his face every moment of silence
since, and what do you say
when he cries at the news
when he says, he is helpless, we
are helpless, these children on TV beseech us
on borders
Baghdad Beirut Amman Ramallah Jenin
left to rot in the
putrid air of war and warfare and the powers
universal that don't care
and what to say, how to wash away the
    childhood
spent witnessing
massacres of bloodied bodies
strewn about here and there,
the women in constant tears
and your mother tried, she tried all she could
    dare
to give you innocence, but the persistence
of memory is such that the murdered
limbs of your ancestry are
always there and what does it feel like you say?

Well,
you wake up everyday
and you wished visas and passports didn't

take precedence
over the need in your center for
the family reunion
and that safe familiar
inner presence
and you spend lifetimes in lands distant astray
and your rights are given to you by governments alien
and democracies you cared not for
with not an olive tree to heal you and yet you
are thankful, grateful, jubilant
even that your kids
are accounted for, asleep in their bedrooms
with their crayons and dolls, and
so you stay, year after year in exile
you stay. You grind your teeth at night, and take your blood pressure medication
and weep into the phone
and weep into the letters that are the only way.

You
stranger on a train who thinks i'm sexy
who thinks i'm American
in my Levi's jeans and blue tie dye tshirt and purple
lipstick, and my walkman blasting the
prodigy, for teenagers are the same

HOME

everywhere, this is where I AM from, and you
you, every single one of you who asks me
    about my way
you who think
i'm young and filled
with mystery and exotic lands
and an alluring sense of oriental tragedy
this is what it is
this is our way
and now picture this
put yourself in this image and imagine away
to be from where i'm from,

do not see your children
for years
if you knew where they were
to begin with
do not bear the news for another day

do not whisper a word when you need to
    scream
out what they've made
you and who've you become
and how it is to be questioned at every turn
about the political activities of your uncle
whom you never met
who ran a pastry shop

and the opinions of your aunt
from the other side of the family whom
you never met
and forget
you will forget that a family is a normal unit
of harmony and people just get on planes
and marriages are joyous occasions not
reasons to panic
and feel robbed of your rights
count not the tears that are shed in nights
when you cannot tell
why one should hold on to their name
and know that this is what it's like to not have an answer
to where you are from,
for you are from everywhere
and nowhere
and you have a home
but it is not there
it was never there for you
you were never allowed to see

you were born a refugee

and this is what it is to be
Palestinian. This is what it is to be Palestinian.

This is what it is to be, and be and be
and
not be.

TO THE TENS OF THOUSANDS IN THE STREETS, PROTESTING, IN MY HEART

For Stevna, a demonstration unto himself.
Beirut, 01/2009

look, smile, observe

how the images unfold

turn on your televised war and

fully see, hour of day, day of night, watch the minutes of

death unwind, droplets of white powder fight

now black, through the sand clock of eternal time,

watch the news, ignore the views, but see

the eyes enraged of people not born

to be

who do not know you, who do not know me, and

observe

hands smeared in red paint to

portray, to say, these are the dreams of our children

HOME

dead, this is the Palestinian
blood smeared on every face left unwept
this is Palestinian
flesh enmeshed in your daily bread

my homeland has captured the imagination of
  the world

my refugee ID burnt upon each
and every newspaper you read, every book
  you ever took to
bed with you, on every page, on
every dried flower, and weed, and tree
my children will be Palestinian
their children will be Palestinian

observe

i am here
and your tanks cannot level that, your guns
  cannot evaporate that
your voices anguished in fear have not the
  strength to stay
no matter how vile
how violent
your hands
no matter what murder they inflict

lost, bitter
what deviance from humanity they veer,
lost, bitter
astray

observe

my lost home
has captured the aspiration of the kind world
nowhere can you go
without embracing a boiling ember of my trace
my just declaration, my
clutched hands forcing
the stance to hold on to our place
our holy space
the numbers killed, the numbers
dispersed, the ones you displace
move on, but we are there, in every
conscience of a woman
a man
a child, of any human living comfortably with a human face
turn on your TV

observe

my families have captured
the envy of all the forgotten cities
as time renders us immortal
Jerusalem there to be, to stay, to die
over and again, and
to be free
my soil has captured the imagination
the deafening clamor of all those
out in the cold and the heat and under the
bullets and in the snow, and in the
rain, and in the middle of working hours, under
tear gas, under police clubs,
handcuffed, voices sour and hoarse with
venom, to spit,
to say,
Palestine is here
the olive trees are here, long before
you came
and long after you have to go away
may you live like dogs
elsewhere, may you
wander again
like
a beaten
like a haggard stray

and you will leave
and Palestine shall stay,
in any shape, form, location it takes, for
my children will be Palestinian, their children
will be Palestinian
and no government in this heinous
world they have created could ever
could dare, could begin to, could
make that
any other way

observe

we shall not forgive
i shall not forget
and time takes care of everything.

PARTYTIME

Beirut, 04/2008

Beirut buried in colored paper
faces malevolent displayed in altars
to martyrs erected
never resurrected
seeped in blood
and oblivion
Beirut what have we done with your walls
we never heeded your
teary calls
and now a burial
and for me,
a plane ticket
your heart beat, quiet quiet
Beirut is alone
buried

CONVERSATIONS/ INEBRIATIONS/ DEMONSTRATIONS

For Saseen, a passionate man.
Beirut, 10/09/09

The Arabs can have as many leaders puppets whores
repeating folly in theater
while we suspend not our disbelief.
Listen to this, this is the permanent theme. The Question of Palestine,
for its people for the murdered youngsters for the elders
is very much alive
the scar tissue in wounded strips still itches stings,
singes a little this skin, late at night when
our cities of exile open up to blacken us
with silence
and despair, the Question of Palestine is alive,
festers the ache
grows
reality fades and we buzz alight, I throw up Indignance. Steeped in Repugnance. Offer my body in
Malevolence.

HOME

In the stomachs of my compatriots of
oblivion, sprawled breathless
on Beirut couches
of loss
inebriation follows us, tells us, it's
alright, it's our right to say
to shout shut the horizon
of this living room, this war torn journey
of my eyes
to yours of chaos, delirium precious, the
scent of Beirut,
dizzy we are,
devoid of focus, and yet, yet we are trembling in heat
trembling in fingers that shimmer in violence
trembling in necessary physical decadence
trembling as our voices pitch louder
to shout over the din of electronic presence
that Palestine cannot die
we cannot appease our hunger
there will be no acquiescence
no matter how much you smoke
no matter what we drink
no matter how much my adorned body sparkles.

That nagging memory burns. The tips of your

dirty fingers offer me pleasure. Vibrant.
Taut with hate, rigid,
clasped around these throats of
shame, those tips that smolder,
choke our throats,
guilty,
drunk,
silent.
The Question of Palestine lingers.

Defiance centers itself between my
shoulders, heavy, restless. Here
in this place of harmony, we remember
you, you who have given us vile pus,
and tears of brick rubble, you who defecated
on the legacy of prophets before you,
sacred,
you who have bequeathed us jowls
irate, ruins for our picnics, blood to seep
    through
these nights of no slumber,
you who have come from across the
world to poison the Jordan river,
to barren the soil of the Galilee,
to clamp down our ever after.
The Question of Palestine is alive, no

matter how many
tired souls surrender.

I have eyelids of steel,
that package this hate, this zeal, this
nonstop effortless ability
to heal, to feel nothing but apathy should we bury
your children,
should we take it upon ourselves to teach you
lessons you wrote for us,
to show you the reel of history, snapshots of displacement,
politics of dispossession,
lifetimes of suppression, oppression, absurd, surreal.

When will you memorize this fact
the Question of Palestine is pervasive,
is alive,
is real?

He speaks to me of your extinction, he tells me stories
I long to relate, tells me among the vodka
and Beirut's stars and her samba
how to dissipate

all this pent up hate, he tells me
fables I long to relate,
he tells me of our fate,
he tells me how Zionists cannot negate me,
how Palestine is here, now, in our eyes flashing across
dark rooms of mirth and laughter,
he tells me to never stop having
the need to commemorate, to
use a gun,
a tree, a tongue, a pen, a rock, a flower, a smile
to say Palestine is alive,
imbued with love,
a world we can personally create,
an enemy we can eradicate, the Question of Palestine is alive,
is shaking the walls with its power,
it says to you, your eyes downcast in pain,
it's not too late.

Everyday,
our short lives uphold honor, in any way
you could possibly obey,
Palestine resists. Affirms. Exists.
And to all you arrogant occupants,
in smiles triumphant,
just you watch

as predator becomes prey.
The Question of Palestine throbs.

The Question, unanswered, is here to stay.

SILENT CANARIES

For Damascus, a nemesis.
Damascus, Xmas, 2009

To write poetry in rooms where youth was
    finished
and mothers died
and sisters became women
and fathers old and weary, to think of all the
multitudes of sentences said between
walls that are silent in their accusation
and torment
fervent   incessant
to decide what to say amongst the lives in
    shrapnel
stinging veins, cells buzzed drugged violent
childhood a ghost whirling in tears and
laughter around
the afternoon fire
we crave harmony in a polluted Damascus
nap when travel takes
not away the wisdom you learnt from your
    mother.
Tales, vital, ancient.

To write poetry is to say it is all always
    unfocused

HOME

yet
present
to say that the clay that shaped this being
    moved to words
now in rooms abandoned is
stiff and cracked in spaces yet inner folds of
water and mud have not hardened
yet
and may never

I am soft
I am soft still in spite of in lieu of in defiance to
    the
notion of forgetfulness and the erasure of
family, resplendent.
To write poems. To write poems.

To miss mothers.

To see sunlight at noon in lands you
    memorized
in absence cherished and protected and
spaces of Dubai distance preferred and honest,
to say I am back in white ceilings shattered
rooms have caved in on our flight, and
my father watches
the resin, the rubble of his progeny shred

around

him, years of aloneness

vibrant, a house decays loudly, a daughter returns, smiling

and still, benevolent.

To write poetry about knowing the splinters in wood caressed

over years of dinner tables witnessed,

a house smells like itself, even unnoticed, even

in seasons malevolent.

I write poetry about nothing, but

it sculpts the picture removed of my mother, magnificent, the

sounds outside the window are harsh, repetitive, careless,

decadent it is this willfulness of Damascus to haunt me,

to plague and torture and to remain

vociferous, cacophonous, prevalent.

I lose words in these poems, they slink

into the air draft through windows

that have rotted, that don't ever close out the streets of

this city, resilient, gritty and I lose more words,

sentences that don't ever end run on in this lazy city of violence,

of forced asylum,

and often, repugnance.

HOME

I remember green eyes swimming across
    patches of sunlight,
and I will take a picture here of family
    remnant,
buoyant,
necessary
enraptured.

I write poems, I write poems about nothing
and
nothing about your lives is irrelevant.

ORGANS ON SALE FOR ISRAEL

For the 215 murdered children in Gaza, so far this week. Damascus, 6/01/2009

Body on auction:

Eyes:
in my eyes are the stretched mountains
of Arizona, the artwork
hung on walls by hippies who toiled in
deserts refuting the corporation and her
    trapped
noose- her shackles- her snare
in my eyes there lovers naked bare on
beaches in Greece, boats taking us from
the alleys of ancient villages with
food and warmth and smiling
to men dancing
barefoot unaware. in her waves, silence so
    rare.
in my eyes there are old streets
in Damascus, dusty, weary, experienced
people who love under intellectual
sieges, and no water, and electricity as moody
as their leaders, prancing, while their
downfall we prepare.

HOME

in my eyes there is
Beirut, my most trusted mistress, abandoned
adored, abhorred and
useless, her sea restless, her people
calm, her sea quiet, her people
violent, and the smell of gardenias defiant in
 the fuming air.
in my eyes
there is Amman, concrete jungle
hiding the jasmines i knew
in other lifetimes, the jagged curves of her
embroidery, brought in by women who
knew what it is to live, and
live freely. in my eyes there is Paris, wine in the
morning, a grimace on every face
in the cold, sunshine on exquisite
buildings hiding lovers
breathless, legs open
without a wrinkle in their souls, without a tear.
in my eyes
there is Rome and more art than
the eye could stand
more flair and abandon to
wrench at me, to tug at me, to make me
sway and swear. in my eyes, there is New York,
 loving me,
a continent of darkness and light

equal, shifting, a morphing embrace
that entangles and smothers and
sets you free in the most
immeasurable ways, sometimes, for the
cheapest bidder, with the
lowest fare.
in my eyes is Seattle, wet, and smoky, and
with music
to follow me everywhere, friends with kind
    eyes
and open hands that
say here is my love
take, take without a word, without
needing to declare.
in my eyes is Geneva, cobbled streets
to wander, fresh breath to
heal, and memories of my mother
whose green eyes remain
partly there. in my eyes is London, parks
filled with my longing
colored homes filled with peace, language
    there
to ravish me, and a colonial history bloody,
and powerful and often unfair.
in my eyes is new Orleans and my prayers
that the roads i consecrated forever are
still there, that the beads of color

HOME

that ring out laughter and the stomping
of feet in joy universal are still there.
in my eyes is DC, barren and
meeting me with a cold
political plotting stare. and in my eyes
is Los Angeles, a porn palace
to satisfy every urge before
the next one unfolds, in a hurry, a consumer
land of magic, a sexy woman who
just let down her hair.
in my eyes is Muscat, incense
to hypnotize me, a people so
lovely, palm trees that shed not
their dates for me, proud trees, trees
that can never go bare.
in my eyes are old photos, of images
unnumbered, a developed landscape
of persistence, and light, and flare.
behind my eyes are horizons
of rapture, and inner
cities of despair, camps
of empty futures, and hotels of gilded
golden arches and movie stars
with easy flair sauntering
hallways of fame and glitz
and cameras that record death with a steady
    glare.

Feet:
in my feet are sand stains
gathered trudging the deserts
of Abu Dhabi, free in the cool nudity
of my toes that unfurl rebellious
that echo the sun, that call out to
the wind, that play and wrestle
and hum
twirling abandon, no matter what
or where.

Hair:
in my hair is the lingering trace of India, cheaply
sought in Dubai
replicas of temples filled with spirits holy and people
in the dark, people who are color incarnate
people who insist they can exist,
anywhere.

Temple:
beads of glitter knot together my
temple, they quell
the pulsing thoughts of
moments passed, throbbing

with memories of places far,
places rancid
places with no care. Dubai, shiny
spectacle of our greed
of my aloneness, of our need
for peace and order
and the quietude in our raging
stomachs, of thunder
filled to the brim with the stench
of wars that always
occur that damage, maim, kill
wars that always occur
elsewhere.

Hips:
in my hips is every woman who ever listened
to the rhythm
of ebbing power,
the syncopation of procreation, a frenzy
of movement unexplained, instinctive, a safe
    spot
to begin life anew
a home for the millions
waiting to enter my creation of breath
and bone and flesh and hair.

Tongue:

in my tongue is the speech of the ordinary, the flight
of poetry unyielding to earth and her gravity
in my tongue is language
to heal all the wounds in my
lungs, and in my kidneys, and in my ribs
and in my curls
the ability to be heavenly
the divinity of permanence in time escaping
all that's ordinary, all that's temporary, all that
settles in your brain chemistry of me, hidden
protected safe somewhere,
the salt of your favorite lover's skin, the thousand
different flavors you have gained,
in my tongue there are litanies, and songs
and spells that
cascade eternal, a spring of blossoms blooming
a word a word a word to capture you. a word
to make us one. a word to say i am there.

Lips:

in my lips are the kisses that stay
and make a home
in the sweetness

the succulent biting that quivers
with breath and madness
and pouts to claim their need to be touched, to
 be tasted
to be heard moaning the voices
of pleasure intricate
personal
compelling your softness
to crush me in lingering motions that tear
that dig trenches in any resolve
lips that
pitch a name on my lips, that take in the hurt
that placate all the pain that they can dare.

Hands:

in my hands is mystery
tangible threads that tie me to all i ever have
 held sacred, from wind, to sand, to clutching
 happy at the resplendent universal air. in
 my hands is the skin of all the humanity
 reverent
i have experienced
in your bodies of gold, in your bodies
of light, in your bodies that you in love share.
 in my
hands is longing for the past, a beckoning
of the future, a defiant stance

of stubborn power, a refusal
to back down a refusal to just lie there.
in my hands is a
clenched fist rising invisible
in every second i needed
to fight you, to say, to
hell with you. to hell
with you. to rancid depths of
swamps of hate with you, to eternal suffering
with you and your government and your
people and your guns and tanks
and flag and ideology and history
and beliefs. to the grave i curse your children.
to the grave i ignore the previous holocaust
    you witnessed
to death and destruction with you
and anything or anyone for whom you care.

Heart:
and in my heart, in my heart is Palestine.
and that, that is not for sale.

CHAPTER FOUR
LUST

DAILY BREAD

Beirut, 02/2008

I thought to write a dirty poem
one about fucking and sucking
and lips pouted
licking
cigarette butts left in ashtrays flowing
about the grit edged into our teeth
grinding TV screens that
enlarge year after year to devour
us with all the porno sacred

I thought to write about the harsh
words we dismiss
the bitter words
we utter
the basic daily bitching
we mutter
I thought to remove all splendor
to strip my thoughts brutal

I thought to describe fast food containers after
 our sleepless night
I thought to show you the bruises I gathered in
 the restless morn

I thought to write about bombs
and limbs bleeding
and eye sockets gouged
and entire nations massacred

I thought to write in words that do not rhyme
that have no flow
words that reek like scum
words about what we have become
you, enslaved by your cocks
us, enslaved by history
by the goddamn army checkpoints
and the barbed wire streets
the machine gun blocks
Arab students dumping art for rocks
burning tires to inhale black death
like your eyes

I thought to write a dirty poem
like your heart

like many others I can name
like the ones who rule this jungle
we call home
my breath to them money whoring
my smile a mere game

LUST

I thought to write about hate
and children dying as we speak
I thought
and thought
I thought through the whole violent day

there is nothing to say

your eyelashes are curved long on your cheek
you sleep
it is silent
and I love you.

SKIN

For MJ, who brought me laughter.
Dubai, 03/2009

Dubai,
the languid days merge into
creases forming on waists
lethargic
the bank account fattens
like the useless thighs
I carry
yet pulse throbs
waiting to curve my arms into your neck
for skin dark
for your hair wet
voice breathless
those brown eyes
not seeing mine
that pitch of laughter rumbling deep
from slumber you
are safely ensconced in my arms
and unavailable
even for a summer
even for the second it takes to love one
    another
even for a moment we can share

LUST

before we move on to
another
consumers looking for aisles of longing
for kisses, hands that move, hands
that tell stories
smoke in rugged
maleness, heat I crave
even when kind, even in my anger
even in Dubai, where
you are my
laughter.

I could not
bear the slow afternoons I slept
the sober dreams I instantly forget
the blank pages of verse unwritten in boredom
unwritten in apathy
unwritten even
after
the days I wept, the days strayed on idle
my face uneven, my posture
unkempt
the nights recording lights of Dubai machines
working, toiling while I looked
for fixes for the woman who
is lonely the woman who is hungry the woman

214   who misses
making the world better
while they make it shinier
higher
faster
while they slather a thin veneer on this whoring
they paint the walls with mirrors
of self respect
and I stumble in dust
unfocused
questions unventured
answers
undiscussed
truth always unexpressed
the disaster of poverty extinguished with too many
cigarettes unfinished, chasing
vodka that flows freely
dreaming
a silent query
who gets to decide in this farce
in this tragedy
in this epic tale of inequality, who gets to tell me I can nap
and grow heavier with sloth
grow fat in disgust

my lips, alone
weary
my fingers restless clenched, devoid of
    rapture, of the pressure
of grasping you lover
empty
like the lives stretched on cranes glimmering
while a postcard hides
the stories of fifteen men living in one
    bedroom
eating
maybe not eating
loving
shitting in putrid spaces
sinning in thoughts they control not
nothing
nothing to show for
maybe tears stifled in hotel back entrances,
    hidden
from guidebooks
fearing
maybe the violence stirring in the faceless
nameless throngs of men
beautiful men
dark men
capable men
men without an anchor

men without a future
men without families
men simply
appearing
as ghosts, as numbers in articles on labour
rights and queues at airports
and jokes in bad taste,
my stomach turning in rancor
and perhaps in a compassionate conversation over wine
perhaps a line in some clean
perfumed
hotel enclosed banter
we think of what it could have been like for those with
another skin color

and the men still move
and the men still sweat

and
I miss your body
building forgetfulness into mine
and Dubai lies humid static buildings unbuilt buildings unlived
unpainted unloved calling to the skies
for a home in the displaced corners of my eyes

outstretched
unanswered
dreary
my fingers splayed, the stories replayed of the
days you were
out of touch
out of reach

stories, like
here is the woman at the beach.

Here is the woman alone at the beach.
Here is the woman
with sand in her toes, grains in her hands
slithering like silk through fingers over your
wide chest, your soft nape, the shape
of the unavailable rounded curves of you
the hidden corners you tuck away
here is the woman looking at waves,
hampered by factories on both
edges of that horizon which is no
horizon, of that freedom which is not freedom
here is the woman who spent the afternoon
on the beach alone
whom no one spoke to
whom no one noticed

218 no matter
the smile in her eyes, no matter the wind in her free hair
no matter what or where
her glances
bestowed love on
those uninterested
on those unaware
here is the woman who was alone
soaking lean bodies of lust stretched
sea, sand, sky and
stone
elements to wrap my heart, as a gift, to send out
with the setting sun, and here is the desultory walk
home alone
reciting tales of love that were not spun
here is the woman who only found solace
in words on pages
unsent
unread
unwelcome, here is the woman who did not
find a home, here
is the woman
still
on the run.

LUST

In Dubai,
dark men haunt that fleeting hand you held
lost in highways
that open space in a city
like a vulgar drunk
spews out meaningless
verbiage
stunk
in the distances
of our palms from one another
my words to you, hung in the air
mellow, and vanished
our voices
unsung.

And I am heartless
and I am no longer tender,
and the dark men march around me frozen in repetition, frozen
in poverty, trapped in my inability to hold them
to trace a finger over the lips that
don't speak
don't scream
don't dare question, or wonder
don't offer a thought on
who is responsible for giving us love

giving us freedom
giving us shelter?

The afternoons of Dubai
are for sleeping, her nights for mindless
drinking
some may indulge in the cliché of fucking
her mornings a burial in sheets
refuting
the reality of this banality
and yet
daily
daily
when new smiles come to me
I am reminded of
how human we are
how simple
how persistent it is
this ability of ours
to be gentle
to be gentle
even in Dubai
where
you were once
my laughter.

I LIKE YOUR HANDS

For a hot Capoeirista.
Beirut, 07/2008

I am tempted always
to fling
my words into your skies
to sling my voice across the moon rays
sheltering our night
apart
always
apart
denied

I am writing this poem in four-season
intervals of an eternity awaiting
your hands
that crater of your arrival
an explosion of internal
eternal damage,
and I am tempted to still dance
on the sea
to lure the shore of your safety
those eyes you own
a green abyss, still
but for secret words I hear resonant

down under
wide
wide

I am tempted to cross barefoot that gulf
that field of leaves burning
in your eyes
that meadow of butterflies rising
you paint with a smile
to find the way to saunter on the tightrope
of our glances
aflame
afraid
alive
hesitant are my steps
I trip into oblivion
with every nonchalant comment I tried
to pull off and tried and
tried
I am tempted to fall
to fall
to tumble weightless in the air
I died in seconds fleeting
speaking the
language in your hair
I died in your resilience

LUST

I died in your silence
I died
and died and died

I am tempted
morsel
after morsel of your lips
that dancer swinging to beats familiar
that cadence of your stride
the lean line
denied to my fingertips
denied and denied till I decried
the thrashing quieted in my
thighs
opened and shut in captivity
I fail to hide
clasped are these hands
a bind
a bind to not touch you
quelled these moans
and drenched in distance
the escape I could not
find

I am tempted to dive
to wrench open that locked trunk inside

LUST

to let the red seeping stain the grayness
of our city
those walls they erected
caging us outside
I am tempted to bust it
fling it to bursting molten
aflame in the dark
alight and
blind with love, blind
with memory, blind and dreaming
blind and touching
blind and
blind and blind

I am tempted to record all the kind
thoughts you bestow on the world
entwined we are in our
pathos, universal, unhinged on
details, that heart you grace
flung apart,
I am tempted to grind my hips into your
heat, into our art and around those veins you
brandish, those
soft moments for me to gorge
and I am forever tempted,
tempted long and deep and wide

LUST

to dazzle the tide with stories
to lure a mountain to kneeling
to beckon astride
that strength in your sun-drenched side
the ocean split
our bare feet speaking in tongues
of songs the stars of Beirut taught us
silent in our nights
and pleasure, the wisps of groans
I now hide
and hide and hide

I am tempted to unwind all
time to incite the
reversal of the moments that take you
away
to move in a circle of your arms
pinned in mine
souls aloft
eyes seeking, betraying language,
our thighs a treaty of desire unfinished
unwitnessed
unsigned

I am tempted to destroy the hushed days
I need

to shed the veils I put up
and string around me
in your words I am enshrined
I am tempted to toss that politeness we crammed unhealthy
unnatural
our lips restless
our tips unsatisfied
I am tempted to prey
and hunt
and to content rest beside
these eyes of grass of yours
you glide into my
freedom
you stomp into my freedom
uncensored, impudent are these
tremors you unleashed
unbecoming
lost in shrapnel flying, that lust
careening under
and inside outside
down, and
upside
I tried to speak, I tried
and tried
I slide into and out of my here

LUST

and now
and I trip into that trap that is you,
I wind up gathered in tight,
I wind up dismantled
my senses
unconfigured
untied

I am tempted to have forever
spied on your
sleep
to have combed the breaths of your chest
centered, exposed to my
heat and need and
all the control I lied and
lied
I am tempted to swim that
length of a stray cat alleyway
cement to jail my Arab youth in vapor
Beirut a city of serpents
I hear, a hiss in the soft
turbulent night
I am tempted to crawl this desert
demystified
to open gently those sheets that
coffin you

in a city that shakes us and rattles us with tunes
of danger and piety and religion gone
astray and
love that seeps no matter how much we
denied and
denied
biding her time, Beirut in
pile after broken pile,
a bind
to shackle the demons in me, to train that
monster residing in all of us
I am tempted to smear it all away
to dissolve the night in my hair, to let loose
the horizons promised in your
smile
and that sleeping form you hide
and hide
my eyes a coal simmering
the parting of your distance hammering
a painting etched in
my mind,
that whirling timbre of a tune
I longed to hum to you, to lay on
your heart, a weightless harmony
a fragrant note upon

LUST

the muffled garble
of all that died in our city and died
and died

I am tempted to ride
the trees to fly to you, to summon
the rays of all suns
to find that one water drop that becomes you, to show
you the flower you recognize, that flower
you cannot forget, no matter how
naked and wet and loose in the sand we are
like a forest, secret
pathways dark and in love
in love we are crucified
reborn and immortalized

I am tempted
I am tempted to leap to you
to traverse that one inch of darkness we harbor
that one step to comfort you
in our now quiet Beirut
her war
her murders and her saints
that wail and roar all the wounds we witness
all our reckless homicide

apartheid
genocide
I am tempted to keep nothing save
a photograph of you
beautiful you
in my hands, in slide after
luminous slide, and I am tempted to dam
all the other channels that were
flowing
alone I am all presence
and instead of love
the prayers I owe you, the
blessings of your eyelashes, the tears
of all my lust dirtied penance
I send you what I
am tempted to write to you,
for you,
instead of desire outspoken in limelight
I am hushed and confined, the strings of this night
are dim in echo
and instead of love
I am a blind woman crawling this page
conjuring a sentence
a scent of your
singular absence, the fingers are exalted and I

LUST

write and write, blind
blind are words in evoking
that wafting incandescence lingering
a perfume of you
I am tempted to ravage
I am tempted to keep by my
quivering by my
solitary late night surrender
I am tempted to confide in you
to tell you of
my laboring heart
calling your name out
stifled
strangled
by my bleeding mind.

ENDINGS
Dubai, 04/2009

1- We promised not to love, not to enter that place
rife with expectation
pregnant with ache
and potential connections that our modern
world despises and
to which we can only secretly
aspire
the hope that my hands were luminous enough
my arms full of light
to catch the reflections of moments we spent, tender
my body clasped across the darkness
of our lives
did not
offer enough conviction for you, did not change the plea of solitude
did not alter the status quo of our loneliness
did not alter the need for another

The lips I sang your blood to sleep with, blew away

the grey clouds we
witnessed, dreary and afraid of the
world growing large without us
small us
young us, left to fend in a place hostile
we were always doomed to be parted
I parted, like thighs you loved to touch
I parted the grey clouds
to see horizons
that were not on sale, were not on offer,
they were not enough to allow the sun
to enter
and geography betrays us
I will always leave you
and religion betrays us
I will always believe other than you
and old betrayals betray us
we will always be afraid
we will always say we cannot love
say, we cannot stay
this embrace a fragment of a night,
    unremembered
it is not for you, this skin
we exhibited
history has betrayed us
futures undrawn have betrayed us

234 moans of lust we elicited have betrayed us
for you find solace
in strangers, in laughter you forget
in smiles only I can remember
and you shield me
from her breasts
from her colors, her breath, the names she calls
objects, the way she
loves to grasp your hands, the space of the way she moves
and speaks and kisses
the details of the betrayal
those whispers you uttered brutal
and it is not for me
this betrayal
it is not for me this poem; I do not wish to write
of your nights in
oblivious slumber
of your nights in another
and you say this love, it is not for you
and I say it is not for I
yet
this here is for you
this poem I write
in the night, in the shelter

of memories lingering stubborn of kisses
before we knew of this
other

2- I thought of you
your body moving in mine
that trail of caresses I wanted never to end
I took that map to lands you knew not
spoken in languages you knew not
with friends, with love, with myself alone
I thought of you
I took this body wasted by absence
by her presence to lands you cared not for
to the weary images to the ancient homes of
    our people
to my childhood and the loss of mother
to the grinding old age of my father
to the question that is my future
to the harmony of
love I found in lands separate from you, lands
    distant
lands you cared for no longer, and
I thought of you when the night crawled into
my bed, and I thought of you
when the sun snatched the dream from my

hands
and I thought of you when the stars told me
   stories
of visions that left me in wonder
and I thought of you when my conversations
   stilted
and when silence provided an escape
for the sadness
that we ingested
into our bodies of heaviness
into our bodies of hunger
I thought of you

I found protection from your glances, from
this love we never protected from
half chances, and the nights were half ablaze
turgid with thunder
the rain kept me wet in the dry heaves of this
   battle I retched
and I thought of you as the skies opened
to let the sky wash us clean of this
rancid daily grind
of this inner voice that cuts off my breath
every night
that lets me smolder

And against that

against the slow decay of realization
that I shared your dark skin
with strangers
against the sharp brittle lightening punch to the gut
there is no continent wide enough
no land distant enough
no retreat safe enough
no matter how high the fence
no matter how far the border

———

3- I smile in the face of
you shared the essence of the
only strings of lust that bind us
with another
and I am curious about her hair, and her lips, and whether she stayed a long time after
whether she made you sleep beside her
comfortable, whether she sang inside
of the skin you rubbed on her
whether she motioned for you
beckoned you to capture the
beauty in her, whether
whether
whether

LUST

and I am clueless, this rampant hunger
will be with me
till I can no longer wonder
you gave the secret of our little cave to another
I am a face of stone
in the presence of ghosts
limbs naked and gleaming by pillows
I thought
we owned
scented curls, scented by my laughter, scented
by our encounter of pleasure
and friendship and that love we never spoke of
that love we split apart further
and now
there is a phantom behind
your shoulder, unlocking the
door to our home, a specter that has evicted me
that has placed my belongings in a heap of rubbish
lit and torched by your need for strangers
and for that
arrows of poison are my eyes
seeing nothing
save the corners of rooms inhabited by my departure
ghosts that see everything you do not

as you stumble through
blindly reaching
for yet another
body to satisfy you knew not what
and in these open spaces
of betrayal,
I force the lips to smile
unlike the
downcast way you
you cannot even open your eyes

4- The flesh, rigid, is liquid
underneath at the thought of the dark
pleasure you carry in the length
of fingers, on me
in the space of arms
outstretched to say, have me
in the stride confident of legs, come to curve
to curl around my body
falling
and there is pain in regions explored by your finger
a pain of absence I wear as a flower
garland to adorn the

desire for you
I carry, I bear, I withstand
and I hunt; I seek out your eyes to cradle me
as a vulture, a mad voyager, as a harbinger.

There is always a sharp intake of laughter,
and a death of a
future unassembled, we shook out our
house of cards
and crashed into the earth's center
unable to touch long enough
unable to find a fix for this yearning
for this indefinable hunger
but the flesh also is a form of betrayal
my thighs are traitors to me
my breasts a rhapsody of cunning treachery
my lips sing songs
to beckon you
as we move away from each other
as we stumble apart, further away, farther.
Memories are etched of motion,
uncensored
I choke in the stillness of this canned air,
in the heat of this morning
untouched, I am spent without having moved
   a finger,

LUST

and I miss you
and I miss you,
and liquid pours forth to drain into your heart,
into your closed palms,
offering
the hope of sun,
the dew of grass,
the dream of an earth cool,
writing stories of
that natural need for your dark pleasure
as salvation,
as reward,
as shelter.

CEMETERY

Dubai, 05/2009

I took a walk
fog slithered between grains of sand
lurked under the foliage
they imported, probably from some catalogue
paid for by salt free water
and everywhere I marked little tombstones
of us, in all places you kissed me
here
you grabbed blindly for my hand, a sincere
move, a surprise in our expectant afternoon
the first morn we drove away
together
here
we suddenly saw each other, saw
really saw
you didn't just look at me anymore, and here
you touched me, felt my waist
my taste
here
we parked to drink juice, an excuse for our
    hands
to keep busy away from the desire to
hold you

LUST

and here
I stroked your hair, saying soft
you smiled in silence but for your eyes closed,
    signals
sent in reverence
to fingertips
hungry
and there, you laughed, the glint of teeth
faded now, lights high of these skyscrapers
shrouded in hazy language and this fog that
    won't lift
from our departure, heavy
the way
you never managed to say
good bye to me
your absence a trail of smoke
I took, on a leash, for a walk. I took a chance
to try and hear nothing but the music in
my mind that won't
remind me
of you, but those buildings, glazed
over, the lights of glitter at the top
mock me, becoming the distant shine of your
    smile
in a big vacant hole where my
ribs might have been
chest dented, heart cavity

empty

nature is sensitive to our demons.

Suspended between grassy
lawn and the humidity
plaguing the trees, I met the biggest
spider I ever saw in this desert, hung
in mid sentence, as we hung in the rift of desperate
messages we never
sent to another in language understood
to end this
to end like the incomplete
lovemaking you left as bits
of roadkill on Dubai streets where
once you kissed me
now,
a carcass bloody, intestines spilled, lungs fractured, brain
matter leaking
weeping into the soil
wretched limbs mangled
skin you loved now cracked open, dusty.

And I stopped to stare at this spider
to say,

congratulations little guy
on your flight
on your escape
on your ability to
make a home out of thin air
and I walked on
without a hearth to call my own, without the universe of your
chest to shroud me
nothing save
little tombstones of your
cruel words as elegies serving
as guide lights along
the grave-marked
way.

ALL THAT MAY NOT HAPPEN

For Lala, who has been so kind to me.
Beirut, 12/2007

i may never know who you truly are
or what paths of secret devil
schemes and voodoo magic
brought your face
to my smile

i will not retrace the journey
to this gift of your arms
tonight
and i may never sleep till death
by your laboring flesh
but for the promise of pleasure
uninterrupted
in your cadence by my side
at all the motion
repressed or broken wild
this promise of soft vapor
is worth a thousand words
of a debt i now
owe

i owe you lines of kisses

and poems of inconceivable wealth

for now
i offer the
sacred nothing i can offer you

fingers to clasp
silence with every morn's dew

a memory of
my calm breath in the night

FUNERAL

Beirut, 04/2008

A funeral
to let the words tumble out
to sculpt a photo of you
in lines unworthy
to rip open this gut
my entrails letters
in blood tainted with cement
blocks around my feet
hands working to layer this charred parchment
in the folds of your fingers and to mold our flesh
recreating the image of you
to let this remembered poison spurt out
leeched by your medieval eyes
dark
like our history
written moaned unsaid

A funeral
I am a carcass of sentences decaying.

GIFTS

For S and S, even if they don't talk to me.
Beirut, 12/2007

send me your dreams
of children on southern soil
yelling out chants to garner the strength
of suns in their limbs
alive
filled with such future

send me your sleep
you who has denied me laughter
your pensive streams
you who has snatched away
you piston body
rocketing in thunder

send me your hopes
a child
so brown, so tender
a fragment you can safeguard in the night
send me then a smile of
delight you could not share with me
an old soul
adrift in my daily adult slumber.

LOVEWRECK
Beirut, 07/2008

It tires these restless hands to row
after row embarking on
a new poem of you
the universe crashes across my chest
an ocean vengeful
language ceases not to fail me
always
oh language
you contain the depths
and i am void
words trickle away with a tide i cannot subdue
pulled by gravity to earth
to her silent whirlpool
oh language you retain within you
the absence of thought
of movement transcendent
and when i am washed up on your shore
ravaged by hunger
language, you sprawl me in solitude
naked
an ancient wreck in the beating waves
eyes breathing in shards
of a cruel sun

LUST

wanting only to
sail a little paper boat of you
on a river in the night
simple
gentle

OVER DINNER

For el Doctor, for his gentleness. Thank you.
Beirut, 11/2007

we are looking for love
in the dusty alleyways of burning cities
in the neon-lit dreariness of disease
in the comfort of arms that hold
and ease
we are all looking for love
in lingering glances that hesitantly
tease

we are all looking for love
we are trudging through rooms like
hallways of memories
we abuse
we are all looking for love
despite our past
despite what now feels like a ruse
we are all struggling
with flailing limbs yearning
eyes sky-bent
our fingers trembling in one another's
while every smile that graces you
is a muse

LUST

is a fuse
to explode the hunt within me
the bitterness i relearn over and over
to refuse

we are all looking for love in
bad poems
and dreams we cannot control
heavy, viscous, obtuse

we are all looking for love to maintain our
    second chances
when we blunder
out guilty words so arcane
when we live each day
thoughtlessly
selfishly
in an apology so profuse

we are all looking for love
even if we claim
non-belief
even if we claim to have grown up
and can wisely our solitude
choose
we are all looking for love in

silences
in laughter we misuse

and somehow love
will leak through our greasy fingertips
binding us
forever to all its
blood stained messages all its knife sharp cues
and in every
luminous rainbow color
in every one
of its hues
somehow love may still imprint your kisses on me
as a stain
as a scar
as a bruise

SEMANTIC

For Liz.
Beirut, 03/2008

she flows your language
while i muttered garbled
poetry in gnarled sentences
long silences
rigid
heavy
she, she wisps around you
her moments of lyrical solitude
a tinkle
a breeze
her own peculiar
harmonic depth
and length
her own melodic latitude
the croon of her attitude
her softness. her ease.

she spoke your language
while i hoarse uttered
half thoughts
erratic
in nature tragic

LUST

uplifted you not
and built trenches
a fort round our voices fragile
walled
spiked
barbwire protected
spells to ward you off
my letters unsaid
left you
grasping at notes floating
suspended
left you wondering
un enchanted

she, she sings your language
and i am the daughter of other earths
and moons and
planets
i make love in a different language
i am a passer by
i am but a precious foreign object

i am but a wild echo to her music crafted

as you two constructed
sentences of shared

magic

i am but whispers
revered in our unscripted nights
i am tales spun in inner fabric
gilded into your
mute inner fabric

and she, she silver voiced
serenades your
sadness
kisses you in places
i dared not
and while i am escaped in
my chosen silence
she holds your hand
on a lullaby stroll of
your familiar language

DEXTEROUS

Beirut, 04/2008

your hands move me without resistance
destruction followed.
and now distance
my thoughts aflame with your tips
and their spells i worship
your hands
once inside me
now from a distance

LUST

For Fairew, may she find her ever after.
Beirut, 04/2008

I have been the savior
of many darkened eyes
in the night
hands have clutched in kindness
giving in to a stranger
each in his own realm
each floating in private water
i have been the midnight dream
and the elusive shadows of a morning after
still in moments darker
but now
these eyes are open in light
and the empty expanses
do not get the
best of me for
these arms are open in light

bring me my ever after
bring me my ever after

EXIT MUSIC

For el Monsieur, who found her.
Beirut, 03/2008

I give up your luminous black eyes
I unleash the serenity of your smile to
hands new strangers plenty
I give up your kindness
I give up your fluidity
and lean edges to softness new strangers
    plenty
I remain empty
you could not love me
there were moments spent in wonder
at the glint of your face
scruffy hands pained tireless hands of power
inside me
there were moments of moans primal
moments of silence heavy

my bed is now empty

I give up your sadness I'm sorry I couldn't
    gather
I give up your harsh laughter, a frenzy
of exit signals pulsing in your haven

LUST

in your sanctuary
I give up your skin to new oceans
and long limbed women chanting
hips breasts grinding to beckon you
their mad hair tempting
a virgin princess in distress
a wanton gypsy

I give up your music
that beating flow we shared
that language to use to bare
to show you cared
I give up your beauty, rare
elusive and specific in its secrecy
I give you up
lover
you could not know me
we make gravity in different planets
the collision of your lips on mine
brutal sexy
infrequent and alight with electricity
is but passing spark
is sheer fantasy
is delicacy
temporary

LUST

I want to hold a hand in the rain
I want the shared need of another in our daily
 agony
I want to explode in short circuit
fires of daily company
I want kinship and respect
and vulnerability,
I want a morning after morning to eternity

I give you up to her
whoever she is

Love will come of its own choosing
love will seek me out
one sunny day
in a whisper
softly

WATERFALL

Beirut, 02/2008

this will be the first
and i vow
this to be the final
hot spring of tears
unleashed for you
gurgling in me
whirlpool
vortexes weep my undertow
but
the water seeps out not, yet
the chest heaves pumping
stomach swirling
eyes shut in inner dams
each organ
is a capsized vessel flooding
hair in curled weight anchoring
heat and liquid
burning
how to staunch hurt
from drooling
seeping
staining my once placid cheek
how to divert the curve

of waves steering
towards these harbor lips
i once
smiled at you with

for now, i am a river of hatred
gushing
freezing

EPHEMERAL
Beirut, 07/2008

What remains of the letters
etched out for you
unvarnished
that simple
flow of invented language
i unharnessed, a wild horse
in our invisible mountain, what
rests, resides, indefinite
permanence of that stain
on this rocky terrain
i plow penning down a
poem of you
this overwhelming silence, what
remains as embers of choices
and my vices
all this unacknowledged violence
for soft they are, these
words of you,
weightless,
a rootless glimmer in the
hush of a night
my love
floats, endless

266 poetry smiles
     fleeting
     priceless

PHANTOM

Damascus, 05/2008

I want to sleep in the dream that is you
I want to stay here
below this empty bed
away from these bereft arms.

I want to burrow under the soil that is you
I want to blossom in silence
below this barren world
away from the fires that consume them.

I want to nestle in the soft clouds that are you
I want to float in that mystery
below this heaven we were promised
away from a land I lost that was never mine.

I want to bathe in the liquid that is you
I want to simmer in peace
below the frigid faces of my war-torn
    neighbours
away from the rampage that is my home.

I want to embrace the eternity that is you
I want to stay there

268   below the solitude of my heart
      seeking you
      seeking you.

SUNFLOWER OF YOU

For Dalal, who is never without love.
Beirut, undated

a flower on the page
drawn there by translucent
fingers in moments
that dwell no longer
a heart ticking above this fragrance

you left a smile in my past
an empty picture frame to beckon
on the future
and the stars have sent me love letters
unaddressed
unanswered

petals form to draw a map for you
a paper awaits,
a flower blooms on a page
and i am alone.

I GIVE YOU BACK YOUR HEART*

For MR, have we been reassembled?
New York, 10/2005

Tonight I reassembled your
life for you. Alone.
Took everything of me away.

Tonight I walked in heavy wind
and sweat
and mud and rain.
New York City taxi cabs
and lights
and breeze and flare
through the circus of Manhattan midnight
I trudged and trampled and carried our love
my soul bare
heavy in my thighs
tears in my eyes
rain in my hair
pain in my arms
honking warning cars
and me
unaware.

LUST

Tonight I rebuilt your life for you. Alone.
Took everything of me away.
Tonight I carried your belongings back to you
a small blue suitcase
in lift lift lift out
and you were gone, last whiff of amber
fading away to a foggy sky.
A small blue suitcase,
in it,
a small precious silk rug
flowers
always in bloom, tame and fake
a hookah
your bedspread- how I loved your bed-
mosaic of color against our
bare skin lying
enchanted together
flying.
Tonight I worked and smoked and drank and ate
and friends came by
to conversate
and we found ways to state our thoughts
as cruel items of you haunted my space
my bed
the thousand smiles, the crinkles of your eyes

etched in my head.

Tonight I took your warmth
your kindness
I trudged them around this dirty city
wall to doorway to street
subway to shop to your face
pain
your eyes
48th and 8th
your eyes moist to see me, hurt and soft
and lost to see me
hurt at this blue suitcase between us
angry words in electronic zones between us
hurt that the last time you kissed
my mornings my breath
was more than a full moon away
tonight I offered you the way out
told you I was off
told you I had to go
told you you left me
g-strings books earrings
exchanged
back and forth
silent looks
my fingers and your brown eyes wondering

LUST

surprised to see me really there
returning your life to you
with care
me aching thinking cursing
wondering why I had
nothing to say
tonight I took everything of me away
took my keepers of youth
lotions of promise and adornments of the temple you claimed
was my flesh
light and glimmer and blush and musk
papers and notes and hairpins astray
zip zip flick flip tuck
pray
oh, painful small blue suitcase
of my nightmares and dreams
of our nights together
of your smiles at each morn of our new day.

Here's your hookah, back in
your zone
here is the lack of me
here is your alone throne
your hookah so gold and large and brave and true
your hookah brought your amber scent to me

         at night
dismantled earlier, broken, edges crumpled,
innards unscrewed
humbled
fragmented.

I put together the pieces
arms legs and vital organs
golden mid-section
a nice flat base
metal to protect me from drowning in your
    seeking face
all stood as tall and rigid as ever
capable, in one piece, complete, firmly in place.
Tonight your hookah was my body
my heart hoping to heal still
hopes in this love we couldn't but kill
knowing this fully
knowing this utterly
as my eyes rake this assembled machine
all its vital organs fine
clean
all the large exterior surfaces smooth
all the metal has an appropriate sheen
till
you peer closely, you see

LUST

little bits and wedges
crumble off the edges
broken segments in small ceramic places
unimportant to the naked eye, unseen
torn metal ripped apart in transit
your hookah
ruined by me
I have no tape, no glue, nothing to fix,
to mask it.
Tonight I gave your heart back to you
and tried to heal mine
I pieced your items back for you, your lies
your life I handed back to you
and as hard as I tried
as silent as I stood
as loud as my heart thudded and cried and
you misunderstood
I knew this fully
knew this to be true
knew no one to blame
knew no culprit to frame
but I knew
that your life will not, nor will my heart,
nor the coals of this tattered hookah
none of it shall ever be assembled the same
none of it will ever know this unique fire again.

LUST

276 None of us will be whole, perfect, and untarnished again.

stolen from a line in a poem by Anne Sexton, purely out of love and without her permission. May she forgive me.

YOUR OLD TATTERED EMAILS
Dubai, 02/2009

I return to your language
those images consecrated line upon line
now filled with absence
the years have not made me mellow
the ache you drew is a scar now
yet
pungent are these past injuries
stitched deep into memories
I should abhor
but I
I return to your language
to learn
how to do it again
to earn the self-declaration of being brave
to unearth how to give of myself what I gave
how to stop that slow trickle of emptiness
filling up the hollow spaces you
instilled within
these eyes are but a grave
and now I, I buried
in hate and stifled hope
emerge from this comfortable cage
this cavity

I, I who was once full
who learnt the difference between your thousand smiles
I cling to my language familiar
a safety net to land on when there are no earths and no skies
in this space of being alone
to say
I can
I can speak again
with
or without your lost name.

THIRSTY

Dubai, 09/2006

in my need to explode
    rests a small language
        whose tiny words squeeze out
            droplet after aching droplet
                lest my skin grow too taut

            and i drown in this anger.

SURGERY

Beirut, 11/2006

I've cut out
the bits in me
that rotted. As for,
the singed pieces, still
holding on
sizzling,
I stomped them out in madness.

I shoved away all the
remaining embers of
tenderness,
any floating thoughts to
render a smile.

I beat down any soft
whispering and chopped
to death
oh so finely
any of my vessels
still carrying blood
stamped
by your
name.

PRIVATE DISCOURSE

To remember love when we were so young.
Beirut, 06/2001

When you speak to me in my language
when you breathe on my neck
and say words in my language
when you do that
I forgive you.
When you speak to me in my language
which is no language
just a collection of words
that are memories
of times
of days
of laughter with friends
of mistakes
and foolish embarrassment.

When you speak to me in my language
I know what you mean
and no one else does.
When you speak to me in my language
and know it will sway me
and use that
to abuse me

and use me
and abuse that
and then face me
and still speak to me in my language
I forgive you.

When you speak to me in my language
I know
I'm home.

When you speak to me in my language
that is not a language
that has no dictionary
no thesaurus
and no grammar
when you speak to me in my language
the past fades
and only the letters
of my language
come alive
burn
not the paper
but my gut.
And I forgive you.

When you speak to me in my language

LUST

I know you know me
and you fill me
with a thousand days of passion
that have produced not a child
not a commitment
not a great love story
nor one that is tragic
when you speak to me in my language
I know
that you remember every day we spent
creating a world of our own
and a language of our own
and for this
I thank you.

BODIES
Dubai, 12/11/2009

Kissing you is
a
deep sea dive.
How are they named? Those long drops with no equipment,
when all your armor is will
your weaponry is lungs
resilient, when you bank only on the hope that legs glide
way out to open water wind sun streaming
to oxygen needed
to life outside, persistent,
to inhaling, to exhaling, to dreaming.
Kissing you is
a deep sea dive, a
pulse, a throbbing
journey
a pilgrimage to quell needing
hips thrashing, protesting this space, not immediate
enough to destination
ocean floor,
salt of you to flavor

LUST

this heat in morsels
the beating waves slap against our teeth,
seeking
kissing you is dizzy heaving
is rampant is whirling is a dervish of intangible coded
letters that have lost all
meaning
kissing you is a deep sea dive
looking for bounty, looking for bones of ancestry, looking
for refuge for seclusion for purity
kissing you makes me a heathen
makes me speak in tongues
of foam
frothing over with desire, squeezing shut the dam
you bombed to splinters all the
wayward
feelings
kissing you is a deep sea dive, inflicted by a world
condensing to become a fragment as small
as this wet sound we make
lips mesh
healing.

Kissing you is a deep sea dive,
and what do they call them? The heavy falls built solely on hope,
the hope enables rising towards light before
bodies disintegrate,
reeling,
the body, kissing you, reveals all its secrets.

There is no hope here.

Kissing you is a deep sea dive, and I am a woman deluged,
a woman capsized, wanting
nothing but to offer you a treasure trunk, a trove of
myself,
a woman intent on the sole miracle of breathing.
There is no hope here.

Rust devours these limbs,
metal sinks into sand,
and kissing you is a deep sea dive I am unprepared for,
a hunt I have no chance of succeeding.

I am a shipwreck of myself,

decaying,
disappearing.

SINGLE MALT WHISKEY

For B, who is a fairytale book of sad stories.
Dubai, 1/12/2009

Your eyes trample in me, solid tracks in wet mud
soft, tender earth accepting.
You stride determined in war zones to photograph
for remembrance
straight-up, hard liquor burning
we drink
to count the dead of both sides of this
equation unclear, unsolved
to claim witness
and I want
I want to wrap my thighs
round your approaching distance, shelter
the lost edges of displaced corners you
flaunt, tell you in heaving breath
how I break
at the stories replayed of nights in cars drunk
following gypsies,
cold, unwashed.
You knocked on hostile doors for images permanent, for food hot
in the winter, soup bowls overflow with

the care of strangers who knew they knew you,
silent. You brought them summer.
This drink heats a hole in my center,
a space for refugees from
all the world over
and I want
I want to bite your lips, gentle,
carnal
not
for pleasure usual sought in nights repeated and
nameless, but for lives to pass wordless
into my lungs,
a stomach fills with laughter.

I am curious at your joy, when bodies spat
blood into your
dark rooms of fog and dreams, in your
languages of recorded
madness. I envy the staunched sadness.
Carcass after forgotten carcass.

You move me.
You move me in ways I dare not define,
a bolt of light shot
surging in paths to trail your history, lone in

that

hunt for corpses adorned with bullets, like kisses

I could expose

to your skin, tight

dry

a morsel of desire develops in

every picture we archive together.

I want

I want to enshrine you in my bed

I want to warm you in the sun of morn

I want to haunt you with the song of desert full moons

I want to weep into your hands

a teardrop to moisten all your impervious surface

and then

and then

I want to let you go.

I have to let you go.

No one keeps a shadow captive.

Like a fine single malt whiskey,
one takes you just as you are.
And like a fine single malt whiskey,
you leave no trace the morning after.

SUGAR CREAM HANGOVER

A sequel.
Dubai, 12/1/2010

Harsh knock of teeth onto wet breath
impatient,
expectant they are these arms of mine
luscious full it is this first meeting of
tongues accustomed only
to laughter
gut shuts off the thoughts of after
your before words promised me
never
now you suddenly kiss me
sticky sweet sugar cream hangover you
brazen you, awkward you
you suddenly kiss me
invasion forces pleasure from places deemed
    buried
after
after
we do not speak of what is after

bites I demanded now wounds seep
smoky memories
mercury hands touched me yet

remained a secret
a shelter?
a mirror?
enemy lover stranger
we do not speak of what is after

but I want open sentences of reason
an ending easy
a destination mapped
eyes that lock, exchange light, exchange rapture,
eyes that may give up all that is other.

But vapor,
vapor you are in the fleeting images we brand together.

My bereft hands shiver,
my thighs quake,
my words quiver, even
even my nerves are nervous,
and I wait.

PRAYER

Dubai, 20/1/2010

I would like to stalk you in lands distant
Gouge out your address from numbers jumbled
Buy plane tickets in secret
Trembling
I would like to wear heavy winter coats from my desert heat
To your cold winter and hot soup
I would like to beat down your fences with Arabic wrists
Etch poems in English on your building walls
Embarrass you in front of all the disapproving neighbours
Shatter bottles of concentrated musk I sweat thinking of us
Wail out longing for you as if we were on sand dunes before Islam
As if we were Greek tragedies before we knew of heaven
I would like to sing Abdul Halim to your sleep
Tell you of Um Kulthoum and her ocean
All night long in voices hoarse and wanton
I would like to rattle your shoulders and shake you into lust
Slam my body against your refusal

294   I would like to weave my curls around your flight
Harness you to all my softness
Imprison you in warm water like silk
I would like to stamp kisses in ink permanent on every vein of you
Burn marks of all my stories into retinas unable to blink
I would like to whisper to you in dreams
I am a thousand years old
And can cast spells eternal which you would not seek to unbind
I would like to touch you
I would like to touch you
I would like to battle you into love
I would like to
I would like to love you.

SPECIFIC DEATHS
Dubai, 18/1/2010

Loss is singular to the details of how many
    words you
could have gifted me
and to the moments we were quiet and needed
no other than the breathing of
walls around us witness
loss hands me poems in nights where even
citrus drinks are poison
and you cage yourself out of reach of
the unending words I want to hurl at
you meaning nothing
saying little of what
you could have swept into your arms by loving
    me
we do not talk of what is after
we do not talk of what we could be
loss is latex crushing skin yearning, I choke on
    the fumes
of what my simmering body could expunge of
    you,
staining all your dark distances with
    permanent
echoes of this particular loss I
carry around like

296   a love story
so singular, so commonplace, there are no words to mourn it.

E-SCAPES

Written on a bus, traveling from you.
UAE, 15/01/2010

These small mountains in deserts distant beckon you

I picture your long legs stride

hands clasp machines of remembrance and my heart is clicked

triggered beats of bodies slamming

hot

this windowpane guards against the sunlight you

could bring into

the flat landscape of your absence

we travel

your body is still wrapped around mine in words

jumbled and dissonant

reflective

did I remember to tell you you are beautiful

did I kiss you enough

these small mountains are your elbows around

waists stretched
moaning
nothing about this journey brings you back,
yet you are in it all
and we travel.

When you leave me the words remain
constant
they are allies in this conflict
they are nets in this whirlwind
they are what is left of your lips on mine,
and I reread poems about you as a lost nomad would
paths that hunt out your edges
sentences to contain you
useless and superfluous, each letter after the other
a map to where you could be hidden
an island remote worthy of your eyes
and my softness, a sentence
a sentence that envelops you
I reread, and reread in repetition hoping ritual invokes
your hands to materialize out

of concentrated desire
persistence
and magic.
Till I am blind.

E-SCAPES, MARRIAGE

For JCS, from his lozeh zghireh, with love.
UAE, 26/1/2010

A man I worked with
for twelve hours in the heat rising
in the deserts and big cars of our gulf
separate
takes out his homework on the endless road home
to beds and ginger tea and sanctified sleep
and studies, quiet.
Why are you learning Spanish we ask,
watching him pour his last few drops of power
into curling lines
new words
new meanings
new language life rhythm music and spirit
my wife is from Argentina he says
simply, answer enough
I am silent, envision a faceless woman he
will hope to hold forever.

I had a lover once who learnt Arabic for me.

LUST

He asked for coffee and spelled it kahwa
always wanted sukkar
he learnt to put the correct h in habibti
he learnt to say help me, ana mareed
he chose to call my eyes small almonds
to make love
dirty words in Arabic breathless
new found intimacy and patience
I call him lover because he loved me
repeating words from countries alien to embrace closer
the woman he pronounced
out of millions of bright-eyed strangers in New York City
he took on a language a life music rhythm and spirit
and today
a gulf
deserts
we travel
and I cannot get you to even take on our possibility.

E-SCAPES, WATER SAND SKY STONE
UAE, 4/2/2010

In the swaying palm trees of our distance is your skin

rough

the length of you narrow

wood against the silk of my sighs

green like the wet memories of first entwinement

in sand are worlds of curves, poems

around your waist in motion

the scraping of moments in travel as

we edge further to cliffs

I fall into wells of lust

dry

an ocean and its gulf is your smile

rare and delicate

I sink into heat we don't mention

this desert is open sentences without you

meaningless alleyways of dust enmeshed in my hair,

bereft,

my eyes are stones left in the sun to melt in remembrance

and the rain of this winter never came

and cars whizz past me
voices
another palm tree strokes my arms shut with
    your absence.

5 AM, DUBAI IS A HIGHWAY

For me.
Dubai, 5/2/2010

Her short ruffled skirt flew in creek breezes of
    paper cups lounging
vodka is finished and thin is this attendance
people do not converge
on boats we visited after late late hours of
forced laughter
everyone wanted to touch her breasts
curves fake and pointed perfect, she was
    cigarette tipped
in this night
plastered a smile on glossed pouts
where those who are lonely looked for too
    many bottles
and we don't have enough bottles
and we don't have enough breaths for these
    cigarettes
and I don't have enough years to keep my
    smile on,
to nod at strangers on boats who do not
look past what we cannot offer each other.

I remember you on a couch, lean legs
    stretched, a face

to haunt all that comes after
we do not speak of what is after
I burn slow with mornings of sheets like jungle
    branches
I burn slow with conversation like water, ebbs
and wanes in streams of thoughts you
could slaughter
and be rebirthed in your arms, a habit
    accepted
a home beyond the rivers of Dubai
dry
with no movement
bodies rhythmic on docked boats
we do not speak of what is after
stagnant like my curls trembling
the heels slip on cheap spilled red wine I retch
solitude and drink in breath of those stars
we share regardless of
travel
look at her ass we say
I'd like to touch her tits we say
she wants to come home with you, he says
lick his neck in a gesture of plea
accept the rotation of bodies in and out
of momentary rapture
they play
and I burn slow with your eyes dark

306   your glances heavy
the weight of ruptured flesh we made poetry
the creek ripples to taunt and say
I sparkle
I sparkle
I shatter at fleeting aches in regions hidden
spasms of physical matter shake
at the absence of you
and there is no love here
and there is no love here
and I drown slow with the rocky tides of your departure.

GEOGRAPHY OF US

Dubai, 24/2/2010

You touch sand
war surrounds your kite eyes soaring out of
　my body
wants to be a harness
you touch metal in deserts
hot my cheeks blaze as the words slip away
we do not speak of what is after
we do not allow in the silence
i wonder what you eat in the morning
and whether you speak softly in sleep to no
　one
i have befriended your
disappearance, know it well, it fits my hands
　clenched
patience burns the edges of my unlicked lips
i wonder what you eat in the evenings
and whether you moan softly in arms
not mine
not enough for a sentence
you touch trees
take trains
ache on plane rides to such faraway places the
languages i rule are

LUST

insufficient
to conjure photographs of tenderness
i wonder what soap you use
who washes your jeans
is your pillow comfortable
what strangers have you met
what naked memories you seek to forget
you touch car doors
leather
passports
and i touch myself,
picture your hands cupping this life throbs in dark rooms
accustomed to distance.

You touch nothing here.

SUNNY SIDE DOWN

Dubai, Breakfast, 05/3/2010

A grey morning stretches my
skin into the pale
contours of the word no
a duststorm gathers in our city of
non sequiturs and
frozen kisses, this damned
cotton mouth I have that cannot
melt your wet chest around mine, this sand mouth
twists around itself, a freefall heavy through thirty
eight floors of lust to the
iced desert beneath my untouched feet.
The levels drop in voices sunk with refusal,
a skyscraper of sadness builds in my limbs
and the earth beneath cracks every time you still smile.

310   **THE RULES**

For all my lovely single girlfriends.
Dubai, 24/2/2010

Never love a man who has not called to
anxiously check whether you did get sick and
    could possibly be in bed
retching your inner guts while making excuses
    for
his busy self, traveling.
Never love a man who answers your
explosive letters with one liners
that lead nowhere,
who wants to rip your clothes off only when
    they are
fishnet stockings and does not
encourage you to hold his hand
in public, never let that
man be your waking hours,
be your insidious dreams in morning desire,
never ask him how he is seven times in an
    evening because
he was tired a week earlier, never jump off the
tired couch with your tired hands
on your tired feet
to give him the ease and comfort of soul with
    your

LUST

magic fingers that heal, never cancel your
  work, your
dates, your coffees, your time
alone for a man who forgets to check his phone
who does not hide in office corners to call you,
never buy him little gifts you see everywhere,
  because somehow everything, everything
now reminds you of him, even little trinkets
he most certainly will
hate become objects of worship you claim he
  ought to have
in his home
without you.
How he needs a larger mug for the tea you
  imagine
drinking together. Never fret about what to
  give give give
a man who will always leave you,
never look in the mirror and see your curves
  through his eyes
wondering if he can notice in the dark
the extra hairs you forgot to shave
the blemishes you can't erase
the three pounds you may have gained, the
  skin
stretches, the flesh dimples,
and never let yourself make love in the dark,
  even if it

feels like the only way,
never wait on him, never wait for him, never
hang breathless wondering what
he is going to say, staring at ceilings while he moves in
other worlds ambivalent,
never let yourself be curious as
to what he's thinking, word by word,
action by action,
deciphering minutiae of nothing to the madness in
your analysis, play by play,
while he books tickets
dinners
concerts
to amuse himself,
makes plans that are a schedule for person one.

Never tell him you love him
you want him
you miss him
you think of him
in all the languages he can speak
you ache for him
and never let him into your room, to come
and go as he pleases,

LUST

to flee and then return at midnight to stay, never
ever deny yourself love for him, deny yourself
food, music, magic, the
sisterhood that is your ancestry,
books and aloneness and your own inner deity,
never,
never have his children,
never let go of your private
oceans and jungles and deserts to chase his name,
and never,
never ever I say,
never admit that this too is a poem for him.

TABLE OF CONTENTS

CHAPTER ONE - DEATH

DEATH CARD DEALER, TAROT READER, I CRY	31
I FORGET	42
CELLO TALK	45
ONE ZERO	53
Y AND Z	56
NEWSCAST	58
GUIDEBOOK TO FORGETFULNESS	64
COUNTDOWN	67
FAITH	70
SOMETIMES	75
Y, THANK YOU FOR THE VISITS	81

CHAPTER TWO - LIFE

OPEN LOVE POEM	87
BEING OF BUTTERFLIES	93
UNTITLED	96
BECOMING POETRY	98
FOR THE RECORD	108
MANIFESTO	119
PATIENCE	120
MAPS	125
VOCATION: REVOLUTION	131

ALL SAINTS	135
FRIEND	138
MANTRA	141
SCHOOL TRIP NIGHTS	145
PUBLIC READINGS	147

CHAPTER THREE - HOME

CIVIL FATIGUES	153
IN BED WITH AMERICA	163
COURAGE, INCH BY INCH	166
PICK ME UP	171
TO THE TENS OF THOUSANDS IN THE STREETS, PROTESTING, IN MY HEART.	180
PARTYTIME	185
CONVERSATIONS/INEBRIATIONS/ DEMONSTRATIONS	186
SILENT CANARIES	192
ORGANS ON SALE FOR ISRAEL	196

CHAPTER FOUR - LUST

DAILY BREAD	209
SKIN	212
I LIKE YOUR HANDS	221
ENDINGS	232
CEMETERY	242
ALL THAT MAY NOT HAPPEN	246

FUNERAL	248
GIFTS	249
LOVEWRECK	250
OVER DINNER	252
SEMANTIC	255
DEXTEROUS	258
LUST	259
EXIT MUSIC	260
WATERFALL	263
EPHEMERAL	265
PHANTOM	267
SUNFLOWER OF YOU	269
I GIVE YOU BACK YOUR HEART	270
YOUR OLD TATTERED EMAILS	277
THIRSTY	279
SURGERY	280
PRIVATE DISCOURSE	281
BODIES	284
SINGLE MALT WHISKEY	288
SUGAR CREAM HANGOVER	291
PRAYER	293
SPECIFIC DEATHS	295
E-SCAPES	297
5 AM, DUBAI IS A HIGHWAY	304
GEOGRAPHY OF US	307
SUNNY SIDE DOWN	309
THE RULES	310

Gratitude

I thank Yasmine for inspiration, and for her spirit alive, always.

I thank my family- especially Babbi and Teta Z- for letting me be who I think I am, however many times that changes. I thank Nuya for everything.

Everyone who has a poem dedicated to them knows who they are. Please know you are precious, appreciated and make life immeasurably more exquisite. And bearable.

I thank Zena el Khalil for faith and sharing spirit, goals, Beirut nights and book runs. A universe resplendent in our sparkly friendship. And for remaining her warrior self, three years later.

I thank Danielle for her art and her generosity (again) and her belief in our work. You are a rock star.

I thank the Poeticians, every single one of you, for reading, for writing, for listening and being such an illuminative, supportive and great group of friends and poets.

I thank the Capoeira Sobreviventes for their blessed community and for loving me even after I left. For letting me come back occasionally to train and fall on my butt. Axe!

I thank Denise Holloway for sharing her home of immense love, joy and unbelievable food. For helping me edit this "mad" manuscript, and pretty much the rest of my life. I love you Nunu, always. Thank you,

Emile, for balcony advice and superb cocktails.

I thank my one and only Amer for allowing me the space and time to sit on his Seattle couch with Farfour and turn these outbursts into a book. I love you.

I thank Mawya for being the kind of friend and sister entire books are written about.

I thank Victoria Arana for much more than this line could fit, and for her welcoming me into her life with such literature- loving arms. I thank Ethelbert Miller for taking the time to call me beloved.

I thank Balazs Gardi for photos and laughter. For bringing a touch of surrealism to my needful heart in this city that belongs to neither one of us. And for doing what he does so excellently. Gud staff.

I especially thank Maral, Wissam, Dima, Dalal, Matthias, Eliot, Sam, Mira, Christine, Sophia, Mazen, Sulaf, Eva, Mahmoud, Gargour, Joe, Shireen, Kim, Wendy, John Zada, Ammo Yasser El Tal and Samantha for encouraging me to attempt poetics in a place many have given up on. For attending the Poetician readings. For liking me when I did not like myself. You are fantastic.

I thank you, patient reader, for actually making it to the end of this book.

Peace. Salam.

www.ingramcontent.com/pod-product-compliance
Lightning Source LLC
Chambersburg PA
CBHW071301110426
42743CB00042B/1136